ART THERAPY
WITH OLDER ADULTS

of related interest

Art Therapy and Creative Coping Techniques for Older Adults
Susan I. Buchalter
ISBN 978 1 84905 830 8
eISBN 978 0 85700 309 6

Art Therapy and Substance Abuse
Enabling Recovery from Alcohol and Other Drug Addiction
Libby Schmanke
ISBN 978 1 84905 734 9
eISBN 978 1 78450 118 1

Portrait Therapy
Resolving Self-Identity Disruption in Clients with
Life-Threatening and Chronic Illnesses
Susan M. D. Carr
ISBN 978 1 78592 293 0
eISBN 978 1 78450 605 6

Art Therapy with Neurological Conditions
Edited by Sally Weston and Marian Liebmann
ISBN 978 1 84905 348 8
eISBN 978 0 85700 912 8

Art Therapy with Physical Conditions
Edited by Marian Liebmann and Sally Weston
ISBN 978 1 84905 349 5
eISBN 978 0 85700 911 1

Therapeutic Photography
Enhancing Self-Esteem, Self-Efficacy and Resilience
Neil Gibson
ISBN 978 1 78592 155 1
eISBN 978 1 78450 421 2

ART THERAPY WITH OLDER ADULTS

Connected and Empowered

ERIN PARTRIDGE

Jessica Kingsley *Publishers*
London and Philadelphia

First published in 2019
by Jessica Kingsley Publishers
73 Collier Street
London N1 9BE, UK
and
400 Market Street, Suite 400
Philadelphia, PA 19106, USA

www.jkp.com

Library of Congress Cataloging in Publication Data
Names: Partridge, Erin, author.
Title: Art therapy with older adults : connected and empowered / Erin
 Partridge.
Description: London ; Philadelphia : Jessica Kingsley Publishers, 2019.
Identifiers: LCCN 2018020777 | ISBN 9781785928246
Subjects: LCSH: Art therapy for older people.
Classification: LCC RC953.8.A76 P37 2019 | DDC 616.89/165600846-
-dc23 LC record available at https://lccn.loc.gov/2018020777

British Library Cataloguing in Publication Data
A CIP catalogue record for this book is available from the British Library

ISBN 978 1 78592 824 6
eISBN 978 1 78450 940 8

Printed and bound in the United States

MIX
Paper from
responsible sources
FSC® C013483

This book is dedicated to the older adults who welcomed me into their lives and to the families, staff, and community members who support them. Additionally, I dedicate this book to the memory of Ellese Evelyn Prettyman and Keith Johnson.

CONTENTS

Preface 9

1. Empowered Elders 11

2. Philosophical Framework 15

3. Just Between Us 33

4. Open Studio Setting 47

5. Connecting Beyond Diagnoses 57

6. Projects with Purpose 71

7. Mural Projects 83

8. Art on the Wall 97

9. Our Art History 105

10. Conclusion 117

Appendices 123

References 127

About the Author 137

Subject Index 139

Author Index 145

PREFACE

The art on the cover of this book is the creation of an older adult I worked with for many years in several different communities. I invited a few of the regular participants to create work for the cover inspired by the focus of the book. She described her image, "Inspiration and Anticipation," in the following letter:

Dear Erin,

My story about your wisdom and help for me:

I had a picture which I showed you—painted, black lines and ugly.

I was ready to throw it away.

I showed it to you. I told you that I wanted to toss it.

Truly Erin, you are the one person who did so much for me in the finality of that picture. With your wisdom and encouragement you gave me tactful suggestions: "Before throwing your picture away, would you like to try something? Sometimes cutting a picture up brings new ideas."

Your wisdom and words saved it for me. I do appreciate you. Yes!

I saved the picture and cut, cut, cut. I enjoyed myself. New ideas and thoughts came to me. New energy came as I cut, moved, and arranged pieces. I began to like my new creation and I still like it. Thank you for your wisdom and help. You surely know what to do. I had forgotten about cutting; it is worth trying always.

P.S. I had fun making this picture, cutting and pasting. I enjoyed myself a lot. Now I look upon it with glee.

Her response is what I hope for in work with older adults; I hope they enjoy the process and look at their creation with "glee." I hope the process helps them to feel more empowered in the world. I hope that it connects them to their internal sense of wisdom and autonomy.

A Note about Language

This book primarily uses the words "older adult" and "elder" to refer to this particular population. The term "elder" is used in many of the settings discussed not as a pejorative like "elderly" but rather connoting wisdom and as a sign of deference. "Older adults" or "older people" are the preferred terms of many organizations working toward reframing our approaches (American Psychological Association, 2010; Lundebjerg, Trucil, Hammond, & Applegate, 2017; O'Neil & Haydon, 2015; Putnam, 2015; Sweetland & Volmert, 2017). In general, person-first language is the best way to refer to people, with the added layer of using the terms and labels the individual people prefer to be addressed by or labels they prefer to use (Ottemiller & Awais, 2016).

Resources

All pages marked with 💻 can be downloaded at www.jkp.com/catalogue/book/9781785928246. Readers are encouraged to download and utilize these resources.

CHAPTER 1

EMPOWERED ELDERS

My path to art therapy with older adults and the specific philosophy I utilize owe a great debt to the lineage of empowered elders I have interacted with in my personal and professional roles. These older adults—my family, teachers, and community—have offered guidance and leadership as they lived their lives and worked their way through the processes of aging. Translating my personal experiences into the professional context happened relatively easily given the community and living environment settings where I interacted with older adults. Working in assisted living settings in particular, I was welcomed into the home environment and offered a seat at the table, a walk in the garden, and a chair by the fireplace. I feel so lucky every day to be doing the work I do with the amazing elders and those who support them.

People often describe themselves as destined for a certain type of work. But how does one find one's ideal work setting, if such a thing even exists? I felt a sense of perfect fit when I found the field of art therapy; connecting to work with older adults took a little time to develop. Perhaps what made me turn away from work with this population in my early career was the assumption it would be all bingo and blurry paint splotches. In graduate school, I worked in a day program for older adults. I enjoyed the interactions with many of the individual participants, but I saw little to inspire me toward continued work in these settings. I wanted to work with older adults, but was unsure any traditional roles in elder care were a good fit for me. I observed art therapists facilitating bingo or party planning as opposed to supporting creative and life-enhancing practices. However, when I take the entirety of my life thus far into account, perhaps my early life experiences set me up to be an art therapist with older adults.

I consider myself lucky to have known so many of the elders of my own family: two of my great-grandparents lived well into my early adolescence and all four grandparents lived into my adulthood, so I knew them as fully formed people rather than hazy half-memories. My maternal great-grandfather 'Pepa' was an inspiration to everyone who met him; he lived into his mid-90s, worked into the last week of his life, and taught me how to be mischievous. When he was a teenager, he and his grandfather came out to California from Texas to find somewhere for the whole family to settle—his father had had a stroke and the family doctor advised a move to California where the climate would better support his recovery. Pepa was one of seven siblings growing up in the Dust Bowl era; their lives were hard, but he always found humor and a way to connect to others.

As an adult, Pepa worked for the utility company and retired with a perfect attendance record. A perpetual hard worker, even when he retired he never really stopped working. He spent the entirety of his later life working with various family members; he built boats with my father, cut silk and prepared shipping boxes for my aunt's bridal headpiece company, and he even did some work as a model for my uncle's graphic design firm—he posed in a mechanic's jumpsuit in a sea of rusty car parts, holding a brand new laptop computer. Whatever the task he was game to jump right in, often causing his family to gasp or hold their breath as they watched him hoist his body up onto a tractor seat or step in to assist people half his age. Pepa was tireless and seemed to have endless reserves of both energy and enthusiasm for any job. The work itself was not the important thing: he was seeking human connection and involvement in the process of creation. He was proud to be self-sufficient and carried that independence into his very last days of life. At the same time, his life story is a story of interdependence—he supported his family in so many different ways and accepted their support in return.

My paternal grandmother also merits mentioning here—a very strong woman who has managed to age in place through sheer force of will. She taught us all about family support systems through her unwavering support of our families—intellectually, emotionally, and financially. I learned my first lesson in innovation from her: when I fell down and got a grass stain on my white Easter stockings, she scooped me up, took me into the kitchen, and patted some flour on my knees. I resumed play and would run back to find her anytime the

12

stains started showing through. She was full of solutions and surprises in our childhoods. She hosted all the cousins for a few weeks each summer for "cousin camp," where she kept us fed, clothed, and as harmonious as siblings and cousins can be. She helped us build forts in the tangerine trees and beat us all in tennis. She simultaneously enabled our free childhoods and treated us as fully formed adults; her proud introductions of each of us to new people made us want to do better and be better.

Grandma Catherine was the sole caregiver for my grandfather through the end of his life—a role that required both physical and emotional strength. He died several years ago, and we worried about what her life would be like at home all by herself. Since the death of her husband and three sisters, she often describes herself as the last one left; the only times I have seen her cry are when she talks about missing her sisters. She has lost most of her vision due to macular degeneration, but remains in the home her son designed and built on the property where she raised her family. Her approach to health is an enviable case study in balance: she believes in the curative effects of a cold glass of water and celery sticks but also savors chocolate and wine. Any gentle suggestions she might do better in an assisted living setting are vehemently dismissed; she tells us she is happiest at home with her dog deciding how she spends her time. Several family members live nearby and we coordinate grocery delivery and medical care with some technological support. It is not a perfect system, but I have learned the essential lesson about respecting choices and elder autonomy through my interactions with her and with my family members as we coordinate care and navigate this difficult situation. She enabled our freedom as children and we need to do the same for her now.

As with many of my peers who work with older adults, my familial experiences opened my heart and mind to the potential fulfillment in this field. These elders in my own family, along with all the others who have come into my life along the way, have shaped who I am as a clinician, a researcher, and a human being. I am grateful to the elders and families who gave consent for their art, stories, and words to appear in this text. Their names and identifying information have been changed to protect privacy, but the vibrancy of their lives remains. I acknowledge my family elders here along with those who have been my clients because they played essential roles in helping me form an empowerment-focused approach to work with older adults. The way we interact as interconnected equals informs the philosophical framework woven through the practices and approaches covered in this text.

One last introductory message comes in the form of a found-phrase poem. I often work with groups of older adults to create collaborative poems formed from words and phrases cut from magazines and newspaper articles, usually with some discussion of the Dada and Surrealist artists (Adamowicz, 1998). The resulting poems varied—some were humorous, some nonsensical. This one, created on a Saturday morning by eight residents in assisted living, seemed to contain a deep message about the aging process, interacting with older adults, and the need for empowerment:

<blockquote>
You know that the umbrella of immunity
has been lifted from your head.
You think of your life as pretty much a straight line
until you see it begin to bend in a circle.
Deep breath.
How soon can I start?
They're gone,
It was far too complicated. I did not have time for long explanations.
There, that's the best I can do.
By the time I returned
I could barely speak.
Here I am, waking up.
</blockquote>

CHAPTER 2

PHILOSOPHICAL FRAMEWORK

This chapter covers the use of art in older adult care settings, reviews literature on art therapy with older adults, and presents a framework for art therapy as empowerment and community building in many different settings. This framework will set the context for the case material and directives in subsequent chapters.

Art therapists have written about and done research with older adults in many different settings, but the majority of the literature focuses on long-term or medical care. Along with our peers in the other creative arts therapies, we are often employed to support older adults in medical settings or at the end of life. The philosophical framework described in this book addresses work in these settings as well as work with elders in senior housing and living independently.

Art and Art Therapy with Older Adults

In early art programming for older adults, practices used in elementary art education were transplanted into skilled nursing. Though these practices were safe, they did not meet the needs of the older adults: "Older adult participants, who were creative, interested in art, and hungry for knowledge, deserved more" (Hubalek, 1997, p. vii). Interest in the use of creative practices in these settings has stimulated a wide range of arts programming for older adults, including the creative arts therapies, teaching artist programs, and festivals; one organization involved in this work, Creative Aging International, utilizes creative celebrations to raise awareness and stimulate discussion about aging worldwide (Creative Aging International, 2016). A report on the state of the arts for older adults in the United States summarized the needs, barriers to access, and existing services (National Endowment for the Arts; National Center For Creative Aging, 2016). The report made recommendations for programming and research, and specifically recommended a focus on arts and wellness, and arts and neuroscience.

Settings providing care and support for people with dementia are natural meeting places for art, neuroscience, and wellness to connect. Given the projected increased prevalence of and lack of cure for dementia, we need innovative treatment for people with dementia in our families and communities. The arts—visual art in particular— may be useful in communicating in these settings as well as serving other psychosocial functions. Researchers studying memory training for adults with Alzheimer's disease found that the use of images in the memory task aided the participant memory recall (Boudreaux, Cherry, Elliott, & Hicks, 2011). Their improved performance may be explained by a finding that communicative images encode in two areas of the brain, a process called dual coding theory (Paivio, 2014; Paivio & Sadoski, 2011). Dual coding theory connects verbal and non-verbal cognition in learning and does not prioritize one over the other; learning is enhanced when people form mental images to represent ideas. Art therapists working with people with dementia often witness increased ability to verbalize or recall memories and increased verbal fluency when creating images (Czamanski-Cohen, 2010; Huebner, 2012). As recommended, art therapists and neuroscience researchers should collaborate in ongoing research into treatment and exploration of dementia. Creative communication practices support people coping with dementia on both sides of the care relationship; a study of married couples found benefits to the relationship as well their communication practices (Williams, Newman, & Hammar, 2018). The principal investigator, Dr. Williams, stated that the intervention aimed to teach the participants "about their partners' ongoing needs for closeness, comfort, inclusion, love and respect, they can make a difference in how they perceive their spouses" (Galoustian, 2018, para. 7). Art and creative practices can assist with developing new ways to be in relationship with each other.

Weiss (1984) wrote about the use of expressive therapy, a best practice with the older adult population (American Psychological Association, 2014), focusing primarily on those who were non-verbal. The literature about older adults with dementia focuses on art as a memory stimulus, communication tool, or as an enriching pursuit (Abraham, 2005; Byers, 2011; Eekelaar, Camic, & Springham, 2012; Ehresman, 2014; Halpern & O'Connor, 2013; Lancioni, Perilli, Singh, O'Reilly, & Cassano, 2011; Pike, 2013; Stewart, 2004; Zeisel & Raia, 2000). In general, the art therapy literature is heavily skewed toward work in skilled nursing settings and work with older adults with multiple medical diagnoses (Abramowitz, 2013; Buettner, 1995; Lewis, 1979). Some notable exceptions are the work of Stephenson (2010, 2014), exploring the creative lives of older adult women, Geller's (2013) work in skilled nursing settings, and a long-term project involving skilled nursing residents in creating a zine (Houpt, Balkin, Broom, Roth, & Selma, 2016). Timm-Bottos (2016) described the need to create spaces for art therapy both within and outside of established settings in order to enable places where "new ways of seeing and doing, along with currently unrealized new identities, will burst forth" (p. 161). As work with older adults moves toward more client-centered, empowerment frameworks, the art therapy literature should shift as well.

Shifting Ideas about Older Adults

In developing a theory of art therapy with elders, I am informed by the art therapy, social science, and medical literature on the topic—both the issues that receive attention and those that do not. The majority of the literature covers the diseases common in later life. Addressing medical and clinical needs is worthy of research and scholarly attention, but there is little to no attention paid to the positive aspects of aging or the lived experiences of older adults. While knowledge and specialized training about diseases of later life are important for people working in elder care settings (Diachun, Charise, & Lingard, 2012), this knowledge should not come at the expense of the positive side. FrameWorks Institute conducted an analysis of the current media and advocacy messages about older adults and found a very ageist, biased system (Sweetland & Volmert, 2017). Some of the recommendations from their work include telling complete stories, focusing on shared values, and providing solutions when writing or creating messages about older adults. We need to "advance a more productive conversation on aging" (Sweetland & Volmert, 2017, p. 6) by changing the way we write about, do research with, and discuss older adults. The theories of the Eden Alternative (Eden Alternative, 2013; Thomas, 1996, 2006) are helpful to consider: this culture change philosophy restores power to the elders and reorients the field toward mutual support and knowledge sharing. Applewhite's (2016) critique of Western culture's pervasive ageism is also important in defining and describing new ways to work with older adults, as is the critique of successful aging by Cruikshank (2013) and others (Holstein & Minkler, 2003; Lamb, 2014).

Older adults are able to self-assess, and may be better able to accurately represent their needs and experiences than family members or medical professionals; this ability persists even if the person develops dementia or other diseases of later life. Self-reporting or self-monitoring practices empower the client and can also avoid some of the dangers of downplaying medical issues. In a study of self-assessment and personal health metric tracking, older adult participants "showed modesty or bravery when facing the doctor" (Beauchet, Launay, Merjagnan, Kabeshova, & Annweiler, 2014, p. 3) and underreported symptom presence and severity. The older adults in the study were grouped categorized by cognitive status; while the answers provided by those with dementia were less reliable, and they did underreport severity, all three groups were able to accurately self-assess their health and general level of functioning. Settings with institutionalized hierarchies are likely to result in similar findings.

The finding that older adults were underreporting symptoms is not the same as a lack of self-awareness or ability to self-assess. In a study comparing self-assessment measures from older adults with dementia and the assessments of their family and caregivers, researchers found that older adults with dementia were able to report on their experiences but the reports varied significantly from the reports of their different family caregivers (Orgeta, Edwards, Hounsome, Orrell, & Woods, 2015). The spouse caregivers regularly rated the older adult care recipient more positively than the adult children. Incongruence between the groups in the Orgeta et al. (2015) study does not necessarily mean the person with dementia cannot contribute to understanding their health experiences and quality of life. The more positive ratings by older adult care partners may be related to the increased stability and frequency of positive emotions among older adults (Carstensen, Pasupathi, Mayr, & Nesselroade, 2000) and the more negative reports from adult children may be due to unresolved grief about the perceived loss of the person with dementia. Applewhite (2016) highlighted the fact that this increased happiness and emotional stability in later life "persists in the face of a culture that does so little to bolster the self-esteem of older people or help us find meaning in our advancing years" (p. 87). The field of elder care can help shift this idea by using a strength-based lens instead of pathologizing older adults' more positive self-assessments.

Shifting practices toward maintaining or increasing life skills is about more than keeping older adults busy. Research suggests older adults with higher rates of conscientiousness, emotional stability, persistence, optimism, and control have better subjective wellbeing, psychosocial connection, and physical health outcomes (Steptoe & Wardle, 2017). Assessment approaches focused on strengths and interests "are at the very basis of older adults' identity development and contribute significantly to their perceptions of empowerment" (Fry & Debats, 2014, p. 1). Art therapy can assist older adults in expressing and communicating their strengths. It can also be one of the ways older adults continue to develop and grow. Art therapists "can collaborate with those who use our services to coconstruct new visions of treatment that focus on the needs and hopes of human beings rather than on their disabilities" (Spaniol, 2005, p. 86) and can work in communities with a focus on holistic wellness rather than disorder and disease (Ottemiller & Awais, 2016). The arts can also be used as part of the work to reduce stigma or address discrimination (Deloof, n.d.; Yeo & Bolton, n.d., 2008, 2013). An empowerment framework requires providers to "forgo any need to control clients by taking on the 'expert' role that puts clients in positions of dependency" (Shebib, 2010, p. 221).

Art Therapist Lived Experience

Beyond literature and shifts in the industry, another influential experience came from assisting with several student research projects utilizing measures specified for use with older adult populations. Though the literature supported the research protocols, the experience of administering these measures were very painful for the student researchers and the older participants. Age brackets alone do not guarantee a measure will be applicable, particularly considering the size of the "older adult" category in many studies, the increases in longevity over the past few decades, and the wide range of life experiences of older adults. In one case, the participants struggled to answer the questions and described the process as invasive (Bennington, Backos, Harrison, Etherington Reader, & Carolan, 2016). Incorporating the responses to research measures into the published paper works toward shifting practice in the future. I have also witnessed students struggle and ultimately redesign their methods in order to meet the older participants' emotional and cognitive needs. Planning for research with such a large and varied demographic requires that students become informed about the norms in the research literature as well as the norms and baselines for the specific setting where research will occur. It means understanding the size of the "older adult" category in past research, and applying a critical lens when reading the literature; the American Geriatrics Society recently changed their style guide to require authors to specify the age range included in their writing (Lundebjerg et al., 2017). Once research concludes, researchers should ensure their recommendations are appropriate for the site; for example, making recommendations for intensive therapy in an assisted living setting with no mental health providers on staff may not be relevant or appropriate. Our culture makes so many assumptions about older adults: either considering them as the sum of their presenting pathologies or assuming elderhood is just an extension of adulthood. In either case, the needs and strengths of older adults are misidentified or are overlooked.

My dissertation research process informed my theory of art therapy with older adults. The study investigated the experience of communication in the elder care setting through digital image creation, individual interviews with residents, staff, and family members, and the creation of a mural with the older adults (Partridge, 2016b). My secondary hypothesis was that large art-based projects provide significant engagement in the elder care setting; I set out to measure the level of engagement with the mural process. Other researchers and clinicians have written about the difficulty in measuring small changes that may be beyond the scope of existing measurement practices (Marshall, 2017). Though I utilized an elaboration of existing participation documentation practices in an effort to record more than simple presence or absence in the research groups (Appendix A), I found the results did not come close to describing the experience of engagement. In contrast, the qualitative data allowed for a richer, more nuanced understanding of how and when the older adult participants engaged with the art process. Several years after the research process concluded, participants continue to spontaneously bring up the experience and refer to the mural in conversation. This set of results confirmed what I continue to observe in my work with older adults: the efficacy or success of an intervention or group session cannot be measured by attendance and interaction during the session alone. Engagement extends beyond the borders of session times.

The findings of the initial study have informed my continued work in the setting and shaped our ongoing research interests and plans for future inquiry. Our work has focused on the use of repeated art-based inquiry and involving older adults in investigation and research wherever and whenever possible. If the inquiry involves a product or industry partner, we seek out ways for the older adults to communicate directly with these stakeholders. We evaluate and form new research partnerships with a heavy emphasis on the voices and participation of the older adults we work with. We focus much more attention on findings arising from process rather than on a final quantitative summary.

Three Qualities for Art Therapy with Older Adults

My theory of art therapy with elders is informed by my clinical work, conversations with others in elder care, the literature, and my research. It defines three primary concerns when working in art therapy with older adults and describes the different components of these concerns. It is a non-sequential, non-hierarchical system, illustrated in Figure 2.1.

Use of broad categories allows for the application of this theory to a variety of situations where the art therapist may interact with older adults. As the populations in many countries age and life expectancy increases (United Nations Department of Economic and Social Affairs Population Division, 2017), clinicians will increasingly encounter older adults in different therapeutic settings. Work with older adults may no longer be isolated in skilled nursing or other specialized settings. Continued application of out-of-date models is clinically inappropriate; it risks alienating older adults and decreases the likelihood they will engage in potentially useful or life-affirming practices. The three categories of this theory are meant to be utilized in collaboration, much like the processes described by Brown (2017): "In order to create a world that works for more people, for more life, we have to collaborate on the process of dreaming and visioning and implementing that world" (p. 158). She goes on to describe the ways these types of collaborations enhance not only the outcome but also the relationship between stakeholders. In my philosophy of art therapy with older adults, the same should be true—the creative outcome and the relationships should be more rich and meaningful.

Figure 2.1 Diagram depicting the three categories of considerations for art therapy with older adults. This diagram can be filled in with the specific details of each group, relationship, or research endeavor.

In addition to clinical applications, the three qualities can be applied in research as well. The philosophy provides a framework with which to address the mechanisms of change in art therapy, one of the major areas for future research identified in the Art Therapy Delphi study (Kaiser & Deaver, 2013). Researchers could focus on the qualities or use the theory to structure methodology. This structure can be particularly helpful to researchers using ethnographic or participatory research methods with so many channels of input and so many ways to segment and analyze the data. A philosophical approach with a framework to organize the confounding variables can assist researchers in addressing their biases, creating replicable models, and writing about the vast universe of lived experiences.

The characteristics of each category come from my clinical and scholarly experiences; acknowledging the lineage of each category is part of the philosophy—honoring and celebrating those who came before me. Working for many years in a setting where older adults' opinions and input are sought after and invited into the highest levels of decision-making has been the ideal place to refine this philosophy. I also benefited from the support and guidance of art therapists who wholeheartedly believe in the importance of these different forms of inquiry for art therapy scholarship (Carolan, 2001; Carolan & Backos, 2018). Each quality description will include a general overview, examples, and special considerations or subcategories as applicable.

Qualities of the space

The category "qualities of the space" comes from clinical and research observations over years of work with older adults in many contexts. The environment where we engage in creative and therapeutic practices matters. Though a spacious, well-lit studio is ideal, it is not essential. Brown (2008) wrote about the importance of the art therapy studio in the therapeutic process and he identified two roles of the art studio space: "Firstly, it provides a concrete form within which various processes can take place. Secondly, it can be used as a transitional object that bridges the concrete and the symbolic: between internal and external reality" (p. 14). Art therapists can tend to the qualities of the space where art therapy happens in ways that support of older adult creativity and engagement no matter the size or configuration.

For many years, my studio was a three-shelf cart stuffed with supplies. Gaining access to a beautiful art studio several years later increased my storage capability, but my practices have been similar across many different settings and circumstances. I arrive early, set up supplies, and create an environment where older adults feel comfortable and are inspired to create or otherwise engage with art. Whether mobile or stationary, setting materials out in a purposeful way invites older adults into a creative process. To be successful, the art therapist should ensure the materials are reachable and accessible, should incorporate inspiration into the space, and should provide both physical and creative support.

Older adults may verbalize a desire or need for a structured project or a step-by-step directive. However, when the conditions are right, they are able to creatively thrive within a less structured, open studio format. Erikson (1988) wrote about the need for space for creativity:

Creativity involves generating what is new, original, unique. We live all too often in molds, tight grooves, and to find the freedom necessary to break out of these restrictions we need a sense of playfulness which allows experimentation and change...the uncracked mold stultifies growth and breeds stagnation. (p. 46)

The flexible, inspiring art studio puts cracks in the mold. When given the opportunity to attend groups without pressure to create, previously hesitant or dismissive elders will tend to start creating. When provided with a wealth of materials, they will explore new ways to make marks and create images. When they feel they are seen and that they are autonomous in the setting, they carry the sense of empowerment into other areas of their lives.

Rituals in the space

The art therapy space should allow for both independent projects and structured process as needed. The need for structure can be provided through maintenance of relatively predictable environments and logistical processes in the studio instead of step-by-step directions for art creation. Session schedules impact the ability to be engaged in art therapy. I have noticed some difficulty among participants when groups change time or location. Even for older adults without any symptoms of cognitive impairment or dementia, changes are disorienting. When I moved all our art groups into a newly claimed art studio in an elder care community, the residents struggled to remember to come for groups and had difficulty arriving on time for several months. Even though they were excited about the new location, they voiced frustration about the change. This can be explained through an understanding of implicit and procedural memory which is supported through "creating consistent environments...such as events held at the same time and place" (Galbraith, Subrin, & Ross, 2008, p. 259). The authors recommended tending to this need through the implementation of rituals. Rituals can support the pre-verbal, sensory-based implicit memory. Ritualizing certain practices and behaviors in the studio can also alleviate some of the anxiety-based requests for structured tasks or step-by-step art projects and create space for more creative practices.

Materials and supplies

Care settings have an unfortunate history of supply practices art therapists have to overcome. Non-toxic children's materials and safety scissors are common in skilled nursing or memory care contexts with the intention to protect clients from harm, but the message communicated through the provision of these tools is not safety but childishness. Additionally, providing low-cost supplies with cheap pigment can be discouraging—for example, inexpensive colored pencils do not leave much pigment on the paper and older adults are often dissatisfied or frustrated because they cannot see their mark-making. Materials may also be perpetuating unintentional social messages. Because of ageist attitudes and the infantilizing use of elderspeak (Nelson, 2005; Williams, Kemper, & Hummert, 2003), efforts should be made to provide high-quality, non-childish materials. Though art therapists need to ensure safety, we should not rely on the use of child-safe materials for the convenience of the facilitator. Instead, the art therapist should be informed about and aware of any risks involved with materials brought into the space and constantly monitor their use. It is essential to notice where materials that prioritize safety may cause frustration and even pain for older adults with arthritis or dementia.

Occasionally, program budgets or priorities may mean the art therapist is not a full-time staff person and may be responsible for transporting all the materials to and from the building for each session. Whenever possible, the art therapist should make efforts to provide a diverse range of materials for every session and not limit supplies, consciously or unconsciously, for his or her own ease alone. If the art therapist does not avoid any "practices that knowingly or unknowingly limit participation by a range of clients, they are complicit in repressing the basic human right to freedom of expression and denying the possibilities of growth through artistic and creative endeavors" (Hinz, 2017, p. 142). Showing up with a limited quantity or variety of art materials communicates to older adults that the creative expectations are also limited. When the art therapist provides varied, high-quality materials, he or she establishes a generous and abundant art space.

Points of inspiration

Many older adults enter the art therapy space coping with medical issues and the negative impacts of ageism. The ageism manifests in limits or assumptions imposed on the older adult by others as well as internalized ageism resulting in self-limiting thoughts, behaviors, or ideas. Internalized ageism can be experienced as a form of trauma; aging in an ageist society means "the betrayal of the body and the dissolution of our place in the world along with it" (Applewhite, 2016, p. 45). In the art studio, these prejudices can manifest in passivity, learned helplessness, and family or care partner intrusion. In order to interrupt these patterns, the art therapist needs to provide visual and verbal, active and passive stimulation to inspire creativity. These inspiration points might take the form of objects from nature (Rugh, 2001), fine art posters, new materials, quotations, and any number of things to inspire wonder, curiosity, or interest.

Qualities of the facilitator

The role of the art therapist in this philosophy is informed by the art therapy lineage I come from, volunteering as an artist in residence with a community-based art therapy program and then studying art therapy at New York University with Edith Kramer and those influenced by her work. I learned to be in relationship with the clients as artists, and that the art process could be in service of so many different forms of human expression. The role of the art therapist is also influenced by the philosophies and experiences of my doctoral education, where we were encouraged to explore the relationships between art therapists, art, and inquiry. We were encouraged to "move into new areas of growth in art therapy" (Carolan & Backos, 2018, p. xvii). The current work is also informed by the "intentional, disciplined, art-based" (p. 21) studio practice described by Moon (2002). Allen's (1995) writing about the role of the witness in the art studio is relevant to the qualities of the facilitator; the witness art therapist "receives and affirms the ever-changing, ever evolving story" (p. 198). The witness role is especially powerful in elder care environments because it reduces the emphasis on verbal language. The art therapist can and should pay attention to the small, simple gestures and marks, finding ways to communicate without words. Marshall (2017) described the therapist "as privileged witness enabling the client to find a kinder form of communication" (p. 59). In care settings, the therapist may also have to be the translator—assisting with this kinder communication getting translated and delivered to the desired audience. The art therapist facilitator needs to embody certain traits and roles for effective, ethical work with older adults.

The art therapist's primary allegiance is to the older adults as artists involved in creative practice. This direct connection to them eliminates the focus on filling seats or creating products, though these outcomes may still occur. Previous approaches in elder care settings aimed to keep people occupied and focused on filling the room; neither of these conditions is particularly supportive of therapeutic work. Many of the existing, structured programs focus on image output rather than creative process. The art therapist is not performative, nor does the art therapist pressure the elders to create any discernable products. That said, their creations are dignified through the display, exhibition, and celebration of their work.

Art therapist as studio assistant

The art therapist ensures safety and success through adaptive materials and monitoring of their use. The art therapist does not default to the use of safety scissors as a substitute for close attention to the elders as described in qualities of the space. The art therapist is attentive to the non-verbal communication of the elders as they create, providing adaptive tools as options not requirements. Any limitation or need for accommodation is approached while maintaining the dignity of the individual. The art therapist may also serve as the external memory for the elder's art process. As studio assistant and careful archivist, the art therapist keeps documentation and records in order to support those with memory loss or other diseases of later life, while allowing the meaning of the art to evolve. The art therapist learns about the elders and provides materials relevant to each person's history, preferences, and interests—this often requires looking beyond traditional art supply sources. The art therapist finds creative ways to utilize objects older adults save or bring into the art studio (Partridge, 2016a).

Art therapist as fellow artist

The art therapist must maintain his or her own art practice and model a genuine, deeply held love for art and the creative process. Jue (2017) found art therapists connect with the artist identity at heart, but consider it a secondary identity. When a connection to art and art-making is out of balance, art therapists may behave in ways that impact their clients—making judgments about material use or limiting materials (Partridge, 2016a), misinterpreting someone's creative practice, or failing to provide adequate guidance with a material. Prioritizing time for one's own art practice is an essential part of ethical and effective service to clients (Backos, 2018) and supports the art therapist's longevity in the field and resilience in the face of workplace stress (Chilton, Gerity, LaVorgna-Smith, & MacMichael, 2009; Huet, 2015, 2017). We need to set aside intentional time to explore and create as an essential part of our work, particularly as new media enter the field and our therapy rooms:

> Imagining and applying the therapeutic use of any material requires flexible approaches, curiosity into what a media holds for different clients, and some technical execution skills to heighten the art and therapeutic interaction (Edmunds, 2012; Partridge, 2016b). Creativity does not live in devices or materials but rather in our protracted interactions of immediacy with them. (Carlton, 2018, p. 75)

In addition to aiding with processing client sessions or working with difficult clinical material (Fish, 2012), it can also be an important way to process and cope with the grief and loss common in work with older adults (Wadeson, 2003). The philosophies and approaches described in this book require the art therapist to be flexible, creative, and adaptive. It is not meant as a how-to manual but rather a creative prompt.

Maintaining a personal art practice and connection to the larger art community also enables the art therapist to develop partnerships with working artists and art spaces. These partnerships can be a source of inspiration as well as creative enrichment. After some time in the field, we can develop habits and material biases. A study of the art practices of art therapists found that art therapists primarily engaged in personal art-making with the same materials used in art therapy (Jue, 2017). As new materials and emerging technology become available, art therapists need to evaluate and incorporate the materials as applicable. Exploring them in one's own work gives the art therapist an opportunity to try new things and develop new practices.

Art students and practicing artists can provide inspiration and access to emerging scholarship or innovative practices. These relationships are mutually beneficial: their curiosity and enthusiasm is infectious and they can benefit from access to a different audience for their work.

Qualities of the elders

This part of the philosophy covers the framework with which to approach and conceptualize older adults. They are the experts, the leaders, the ones in charge. They determine the course of action and they are supported in their decisions. Whenever possible, they are encouraged to share skills with each other, serving as mentors and support for their peers. They are welcomed into the space to create or to observe. As appropriate, the older adults are involved in decisions about purchasing new materials and establishing the structure of the groups. When interacting with collaborators, the elders are introduced as active participants and artists, not as passive recipients of programming. Above all, the elders are artists in the art studio space, whether they create or not. Artists engaged in social practices, as described by Thompson (2015), are useful models for how to frame older adults as artists. Interaction with artwork and artists engaged in social aesthetics, like Rirkrit Tiravanija's cooking projects (Guggenheim, 2018), informed my approach to interactions with older adults in the studio. Experiences like these broadened my understanding of creative community and the definitions of art. Though sharing one of Tiravanija's meals did not result in a framed painting, the stories from the experience are vivid in my mind years later. Artists interested in social aesthetics place emphasis on interpersonal interactions and "embrace the realities of the lived world outside the museum" (Thompson, 2015, p. 19). The lived world is very important in art therapy practices with older adults.

When working with older adults with dementia, their creative output should be considered as an extension of their evolving person-hood—a personhood not dependent on maintenance of previous levels of functioning or the ability to age successfully (Cruikshank, 2013; Lamb, 2014). Though their marks may not result in discernable subject matter or contain linear narrative, the process of creating should be given just as much time, space, and attention as offered to people without a dementia diagnosis. Artists have an empowered history of resisting compliance with linear structure and creating work with ambiguous meaning: "The right not to be clear offers a tremendous kind of freedom: in a world that always wants something from us, isn't it appealing to make something that makes sense to no one?" (Thompson, 2015, p. 39). When we provide space for older adults to create work without requiring linear meaning-making, we empower them to claim this same creative freedom. In order to facilitate this level of expression, we need to provide more than the typical craft materials frequently used in memory care settings. Older adults with dementia benefit from a range of materials and may be able to communicate more through their visual images than their verbal interactions. The art studio space can become a place where these elders, like the adults with disabilities described by Marshall (2017), are seen in a completely different way: capable, autonomous, and creative. They are able to exercise individual choice as a means of personal empowerment (Shebib, 2010). Cognitive status should inform the facilitator about potential safety risks but should not preclude access to high-quality materials.

Synthesis of the qualities

Each of the individual qualities influence and support the others. For example:

- The elders are members of a creative community and they are supported in peer-to-peer interaction via qualities of the facilitator and qualities of the space.

- The room is set up in such a way as to encourage communication or the facilitator introduces a group project to encourage connection between memory care residents.

- In individual art therapy at a person's bedside, the materials and facilitator's approach can offset the less-than-ideal qualities of the setting.

Other art therapists have discussed this type of approach when studying the role of silence in the therapeutic space: "The artwork, art materials and artistic methods in the art therapy room provide a therapeutic space in which the therapist and the client can move together towards a calm silence" (Regev, Kurt, & Snir, 2016, p. 87). The qualities may be emphasized or prioritized differently depending on the unique circumstances of each art therapy setting, client, and art therapist, but in all situations, the three qualities are in relationship to each other. This philosophy can be utilized to structure a single session or ongoing art therapy groups, and can be adjusted to the needs and preferences of older adults across the spectrum of aging experience. The philosophy and use of the three qualities inform the case material and suggested directives in this book. The directives are meant as suggestions and should be adapted and changed in ways that are applicable to the population the art therapist is working with and in response to the clients' needs, interests, and abilities.

CHAPTER 3

JUST BETWEEN US

This chapter covers work with older adults in individual art therapy. It focuses on the ways individual art therapy can promote feelings of resilience, mastery over life experiences, and new levels of understanding. It includes several case examples and useful directives for different stages of later life including early retirement, assisted living age, and end of life.

The three categories of qualities—those of the space, those of the facilitator, and those of the older adults—are somewhat easier to control and adjust when in individual art therapy. Some qualities of the space to keep in mind are related to positioning of tables and chairs for ease of use and light. Adaptations for materials can include both material choices and modifications to materials to facilitate ease of expression. Incorporating materials and inspiration relevant to each specific person can be achieved by thoughtful consideration of each person's life history, interests, medical status, and current setting when selecting and providing collage material or ephemera.

Who Am I Without Her?

A year after her mother died, when all the cleaning and organizing was complete and she and her sister had cleared out their mother's former apartment, Donna expressed symptoms suggesting complicated grief. Though grieving is "multidimensional, often encompassing different types of emotions" (Bonanno et al., 2007, p. 342) symptoms of complicated grief can extend far beyond the expected grieving process (Hensley, 2006). Complicated grief is characterized as different from bereavement-induced depression and anxiety, and often results in long-term interruption to activities of daily living and functioning levels (Prigerson et al., 1995). Those experiencing complicated grief may experience increased incidences of physical health problems, anxiety, depression, and suicidal thoughts and actions (Hensley, 2006). For older adults, who may be at a higher risk for complicated grief, treatment often involves addressing multiple losses, diminished social support, and internalized stigma about seeking treatment (Ghesquiere, 2014). Given the implications and prevalence of grief and loss experiences among the older adult population, mental health providers should be universally employed in assisted living or other settings with high concentrations of older adults—unfortunately it is not common practice.

Donna sought art therapy to address her grief as well as for personal growth. Donna loved her mother, but had many unanswered questions and unresolved feelings about their relationship. A few months into retirement, she was also coping with her own sense of mortality. Consistent with symptoms of complicated grief, she described feeling disbelief about the loss as well as invasive and overwhelming anger at her mother. Donna attended individual art therapy in my studio over the course of several months. After an initial intake and discussion of her goals for individual art therapy, we agreed on a schedule and talked about process. The sessions were two hours in length: the longer sessions enabled her to engage in the creative process and work with several topics over the course of each session. When possible, longer session duration supports older adults' need for more processing time (Gosselin & Gagné, 2011; Williams, 2013), relaxation, and possible need for breaks or rest. Most older adults experience a slowed response time, and with or without cognitive impairment they benefit from slowing down communication rhythms (Kerchner et al., 2012). Because of the intensity of emotion and the content Donna wanted to explore in art therapy, I suggested she create a book. The portability and containment of a book form (Chilton, 2007; Partridge, 2010, 2011) lends itself well to the difficult work of processing grief. Donna agreed enthusiastically, particularly because she felt moderately nervous about her artistic skill level and thought a book sounded "safe."

Preparing the space

When I set up for our session each week, I set out basic mark-making tools, watercolor and acrylic paint, scissors, and adhesives. I included some additional special materials each week as well, such as fabric, ribbon, fancy paper, or other items to provide creative stimulation. For our first several sessions, I set out some published art journals with pages marked as examples of incorporating emotional imagery with words (Eldon & Eldon, 1997; Harrison, 2000; Jernigan, 1999) for her to look through. Donna also brought a box of ephemera from her mother's things: some photographs, a jar of buttons, some of her writing: "I don't know if I will use these or not, but I thought it might help to have some of her things here." I encouraged her to bring anything she might want to include and to ask for other materials as needed. We worked together at the studio table facing out into the garden. Our sessions were quiet and contemplative, occasionally accompanied by chirping birds outside.

Fetal imagery

In our first session, Donna selected paper and created her book. We worked with a modified accordion format in order to create a sturdy book with pages that open to a flat surface for creating. Donna chose to incorporate colored art paper as well as pages torn from old books. She also set aside other images and words she came across in my big box of paper as items for potential inclusion in her book. The assembled book was large with a heavy cardboard cover. She tied a long ribbon to each side, which she wrapped around the book several times at the end of our session. Each subsequent session began with the ritual of unwrapping the ribbon and opening the book and then it was wrapped up again before closing for the day. This ritual, similar to the "rhythmic or patterned movement or vocalization" (p. 21) described by Dissanayake (1995a), may have helped her transition into and out of the work and to soothe the difficult emotions stirred up during the session. The wrapping and unwrapping process also served to provide a structure to an otherwise very unstructured time—her transition into retirement along with the time freed up through not needing to oversee her mother's care felt both expansive and terrifying.

As she assembled her book, Donna placed a page from a human anatomy text near the beginning; the page had an illustration of a fetus in the womb and it was one of the first pages she selected to work on. She did not speak much in the first hour of the session, but then asked for some red thread or yarn "for my umbilical cord." Her use of the possessive signaled to me that she might identify as the fetus in the image. I wondered about her decision to start from the very earliest part of the mother–daughter relationship instead of the more current experience of grief and loss. Her subsequent creative choices and words answered some of my questions. She glued one end of the thread to the fetus and then encircled the fetal body with several layers of red thread lines. She filled the rest of the page with thick layers of dark acrylic paint. As she worked, she described not feeling connected to her mother when she was a child: "We had everything we needed, but not the love and care of a mother." Part of what she seemed to be missing was the connection to the maternal figure. The choice of fetus imagery as opposed to the newborn baby on the same book page was an extension of her words— the fetus image depicted the presence of protection and nourishment but not the longed-for human contact and love. Donna continued using the red threads on subsequent pages, sometimes stitching through from one side to the next; the thread "umbilical cord" searching for a connection point. She used the early art therapy sessions to explore her feelings about the loss of a relationship she never had.

Another thing I wondered about in our early sessions was the envelope of family photographs she brought with her. The big envelope read "family photos" on the outside, but there were no photographs of Donna and her sibling in childhood, or any of the family together; the photographs were all of individuals. Donna ended up not using any of her personal images in the book, preferring instead to use found imagery from old books and a few vintage photographs from around the time period when her mother would have been a little girl. It may have been too painful to incorporate her actual family images directly—the vintage photos were able to simulate her family. Providing culturally and individually relevant material is important in work with all populations. With older adults, it can stimulate memories or unlock unexpressed emotions.

The book as a body

As her art therapy sessions progressed, her book became a rich, textured art object with a corporeal presence; it creaked and cracked when opened, the pages were rippled and wrinkled, and all the layers made it very heavy. Donna's behavior toward this object felt almost maternal or nurse-like, the book her child or patient. The fetus image evolved in meaning throughout our work on the book, much as it has through art history (Menon, 2004). In later sessions, Donna returned to the fetus image. She used it to process additional feelings about her mother, as well as her own decision to not have children, her transition into retirement, the birth of her newly discovered artist identity, and questions about life and mortality. For Donna, creating this book became so much more than saying goodbye to her mother. The work was also a welcoming in of new identity. When the book was complete, she expressed feeling ready to move forward in life. She signed up for some adult education drawing classes and was excited to continue with her art practice. I asked where she planned to keep the book, but she did not have a specific place in mind. I encouraged her to find it a safe, secure spot where she could revisit it if needed. Several years later, she checked in to let me know visual art was a part of her everyday life; she was exploring both drawing and sculpture as outlets for her ideas and emotions.

Modified accordion bound book

This style of binding has several benefits—it is relatively easy to create, it allows for flexibility and adaptation, and it results in a book without gutters; the image can cover the entirety of the double-page spread. It also allows clients to create pages one at a time and assemble the book later if desired.

Materials

- Paper for book pages.

- Adhesive that will not wrinkle, such as permanent glue sticks, PVA glue, or double-stick tape.

- Heavy cardboard or book board for covers.

- Fabric for spine if desired.

- Ribbons, buttons, beads, and other embellishments.

- Envelope or portfolio for items to be incorporated.

Process

Have the client select the paper for the book. The paper should all be cut to the same dimensions, but can be different weights and textures.

Fold each page in half, being careful to fold pages so that the corners meet. Some older adults, depending on their cognitive status and fine motor control, may need assistance with this step.

Organize the pages in the desired order for the book. If the client has selected plain paper of all the same type, skip this step.

Apply adhesive to the edge of the first page and glue it to the second page, lining up the corners. Continue in this manner until all the pages are glued together. Be sure to align the folded edges as neatly as possible—doing so will ensure the book opens well and will have a stable spine. The glued edges can be trimmed after the glue dries if desired.

Once pages are assembled, the book can be used as is, or hard covers can be added.

Fabric or ribbon can be glued at the spine to keep the book from unfolding completely.

"I Never Knew It Had a Name"

Alberte did not move to assisted living willingly and she did not enter art therapy as an artist—she came to me out of near desperation. A week after she moved in, we interacted in a non-art therapy group. She stayed afterwards to thank me for facilitating introductions to the other group members. Alberte broke down into tears as we talked; between sobs, she told me it was not her plan to come to California. She had "planned to die in the colors of the Southwest." As we talked, I assessed her for suicidal ideation and came to understand that she was not actively seeking to end her life, she just imagined herself aging in place in the beautiful sunrises and sunsets of the land she loved. Her eyes lit up as she described her small home surrounded by red earth and blue sky. After we talked a while longer, I invited her to stop by my office anytime to look at photos of her home state.

Open door policy

The qualities of the facilitator were most relevant in my work with Alberte. I provided psychoeducation as well as inspiration. Working with her required a significant relaxation of some therapeutic norms—not applicable to all settings but a near necessity for effective work in assisted living. Particularly for people who were not interested in or appropriate for general group settings, I invited them to come to my office whenever they liked and I kept materials and inspiration there. Some of these residents were much more likely to drop by my office than come to the art studio. This open door approach and lower-risk environment empowered some older adults to transition into the open studio groups over time.

Alberte came to my office frequently; her room was just down the hall from my office. She would stop in, eyes filled with tears, and as we talked and looked at images of sunrise over Southwestern landscapes, she would start smiling and report she could "carry on through the rest of the day." As we continued to work together, I built up a slide show of photography of art incorporating both Southwestern motifs and abstract work with the colors she loved. She also liked to imagine aloud what Georgia O'Keefe's aging process was like, with access to the beautiful land in New Mexico. She described our time together as an antidote to the rest of life. She frequently stated she felt no sense of pleasure in anything, describing the food as dust, the gardens in gray tones, and the people around her as uninteresting and unattractive. I wrote the word "anhedonia" on a piece of paper and pulled up the definition to read aloud. Anhedonia is the loss of pleasure in things that were previously experienced as pleasurable or enjoyable (Fawcett, Clark, Scheftner, & Gibbons, 1983); neurological research has linked this loss of pleasure to brain activity in response to emotionally laden stimuli (Keedwell, Andrew, Williams, Brammer, & Phillips, 2005). Alberte's eyes opened wide and she repeated the word in a low tone: "Anhedonia… I never knew there was a name for it." She repeated the word several times, memorizing the sound of it. Then she folded the paper and put it into her pocket.

Recent research about emodiversity suggests having increased vocabulary to describe and discuss emotions may support increased emotional wellness. Emodiversity is the "variety and relative abundance of emotions" (Quoidbach et al., 2014, p. 2057) an individual experiences and is able to label. Quoidbach et al. (2014) hypothesized that emodiversity may decrease the severity of disorders like depression and anxiety because the person feels the emotions involved in those disorders with less intensity when the feelings are spread across several discretely labeled emotional states; they suggested future research into this idea. A study of the relationship between emodiversity and inflammation found a reduction in systemic inflammation among participants who reported higher diversity of daily positive emotions (Ong, Benson, Zautra & Ram, 2017). Alberte's connection to the newly learned word for her experience allowed her to be more precise and reassured her that her experiences were shared with others. White (2002) utilized diagnostic labels and client-selected words for symptoms and behavior in a narrative approach, an approach focused on strengths and inviting the client to direct treatment processes. The work with Alberte followed a similar progression.

After the initial connection with the word, our sessions shifted focus to exploring her experience of anhedonia. I invited her to use art materials to assist her in describing her experience of anhedonia as well as to self-soothe and care for her feelings of "gray" and "blank." Often the sessions centered around writing the word on paper (Figure 3.1).

Figure 3.1 One of Alberte's written versions of the word Anhedonia in response to the words "my feelings" I had written on the paper before she arrived.

We used charcoal, watercolor, and graphite in our search for just the right shades of gray to illustrate her experiences. Paradoxically, the more we discussed and created about her lack of emotion, the greater facility she had with assigning emotion-words to experiences; her verbal emotional vocabulary expanded. Increased verbal and visual emodiversity might have similar implications as the findings of the initial research about benefits of emodiversity (Quoidbach et al., 2014). Increasing her comfort with different expressive materials also soothed the distress she felt about her shaky handwriting and declining cognitive sharpness—art therapy strengthened her other expressive tools.

Paper Gardens

Maryanne moved into the independent living apartments of a continuing care retirement community when her husband needed memory care; she lived there for several years as his condition advanced. An avid gardener, her apartment had a small outdoor space with a garden where she planted annuals and bulbs; she was known for her gardening throughout the community. She was very well liked by residents and staff, often hosted lunch for new or prospective residents, and was on the ad hoc welcome committee for the community. A few months after her husband died, she had a stroke. Though it did not cause any permanent paralysis, the stroke impacted the functioning of several of her internal organs, her cognition, and her emotions. Maryanne had a lifelong history of depression as well as a family history of serious mental illnesses; the stroke made her depression far worse. She was frequently tearful and angry. Occasionally she retreated to her room for days at a time in a near-catatonic state. When asked or invited, Maryanne stated she had no interest in continued pursuit of her interests and she isolated herself from her peers. The isolation paired with increased physical care needs prompted her family to move her from independent living into assisted living. The move was necessary for her safety and wellbeing, but the stress of the change exacerbated the depression. Losing her garden and her independence was a final blow to her emotional state.

Maryanne's private caregiver began encouraging her to come to our open studio and to meet with me individually. At first, she expressed no interest in creating art; she would walk through the art studio and say hello to everyone but leave quickly. She would stay longer in my office, but mostly to admire my plants and look out of the windows. Gradually, she began to pause over stacks of magazines or other supplies. She had an eye for color and would sift curiously through the scraps of fabric and paper. She spent more time looking when it was just the two of us in the studio or my office together. As she felt more comfortable in the creative settings, she began arranging scraps of paper in quilt or mosaic-like patterns. As she worked, we discussed gardening, and we discovered we both loved to shop at a nursery in the area famous for rare and unusual annuals. I obtained their mail order catalogue, which I added to the pile of collage materials for her.

The qualities of an artist-gardener

In tending to Maryanne as a person, I approached her as someone still active, able, and capable of processing the losses she experienced. The flower catalogue was a turning point. When she discovered it on the top of the stack of supplies, she smiled with recognition and sat up tall in her chair. I handed her scissors and invited her to cut out everything she would plant if she still had her garden. This invitation was risky given her still-severe depression, but given her response to the conversations we had about the nursery, I felt confident she would respond well. She cut out nearly every flower from the catalogue—all that remained were three staples and some tattered pages. When she returned to the studio after lunch for the group session, the woman sitting next to her laughed and said it looked like she needed some glue and offered to share it. Maryanne declined the offer and continued to shuffle through the images. These individual and group sessions were the most active I had seen her, but she was not yet ready to create. She organized her images with satisfaction; as we cleaned up at the end of the studio session, she put the collage material into an envelope. For someone who had every other choice decided for her, the decision to create or not was essential. The interactions she started having in the studio initiated the process of reconnecting with her peers. As she stayed longer in the studio and began exploring the materials, her peers encouraged her to save things or to watch what they were doing—inviting her into their creative processes and helping her feel part of the group. In our individual sessions, we explored simple mark-making to build up her confidence as well as experimenting with arranging her collage materials into different compositions. My role as studio assistant supported her development as an artist.

Transition to active artist

One day, I encouraged her to save her composition by gluing it down. At this point, she made a big transition from passive to active artist and member of the creative community. Maryanne's first piece incorporated fabric, paper, and collage elements (Figure 3.2).

Figure 3.2 This early collage garden incorporated fabric, collage, and acrylic paint. The entire composition is in orange, green, and yellow. In later work, she began exploring more mark-making techniques and more diversified color palettes.

The piece took several sessions to complete and she was very proud of it when she finished. As Maryanne continued collage gardening, she became increasingly able to connect with her peers when she came into the studio. She laughed again. She would come find us in the studio when her caregiver was late in assisting her or come visit me in my office when we did not have a scheduled group. "I am on the loose," she would say with a laugh, acknowledging that she was not supposed to walk around unaccompanied. The paper gardens she created became less about matching color and more about her personal history; she created images about the farm where she grew up, a favorite memory from the home where she raised her children, and most poignantly, an abstract composition incorporating a tracing from her hand and her visiting son's hand. As she became more active, she relied less on individual meetings in my office and came into the art studio ready to create. She went from despair and isolation to becoming my most regular companion in the art studio. Her sense of humor and warm personality reemerged. She also became better able to work with her experiences of grief.

Maryanne's journey in art therapy was one of my most powerful triumphs in assisting someone in the transition from passivity to empowerment: she used the art process to reclaim her past and her present moment via decision-making and personal expression. One day, as we talked about the mountain range near where she grew up, she had tears in her eyes. She told me she was missing the shape of the mountain. She and I worked together, looking at a photograph of the mountain, to recreate the shape on paper. She added a bright blue sky and a collage of flowers and grasses below. Tears streamed down her cheeks as she said, "I have it again! The mountain is mine again." Her images brought her experiences into the current moment.

Collage gardening

For older adults in many care settings, access to gardens and nature may be limited. Directives using nature as inspiration or subject matter offer some of the benefits from natural environments (Atkins & Williams, 2007; Davis & Atkins, 2009; Kopytin & Rugh, 2016), especially spending time interacting with bright colors and interesting textures. They can also invite discussions about different plants and animals as well as assist in planning for increased access to nature.

Materials

- Gardening magazines, books, and catalogues. Bulb, seed, and flower catalogues are a great resource because they often showcase the flowers, fruits, and vegetables in the images.

- Patterned paper in a variety of colors and textures.

- Pressed flowers and leaves.

- Fabric scraps and other materials.

Process

Invite older adult clients to look through the materials and select the natural items they would like to include in their garden. I sometimes preface this invitation by engaging in a conversation about what type of nature they are interested in: flower gardens, food-producing gardens, orchards, or "wild" nature.

After they select their plants, I encourage them to "plant" their selections in a garden. To adapt this directive for people with more advanced dementia, I put tape on the back of pre-cut images to eliminate the need for the extra steps involved with using glue.

When the image is complete, I invite them to discuss what kind of tending their garden needs, what the climate is like, and where they like to be when they visit their garden. We also discuss when they have had experiences in gardens like the one they depicted.

This image can serve as a stimulus for future discussions, ongoing therapy, and additional creative expression. For example, it can be interesting to explore what the garden looks like in all four seasons.

Janice's Words as a Record of Life

Janice was one of the first older adults with dementia I met with both individually and in group settings. She was small yet very strong; even as she walked around the memory care floor with a walker, her athleticism showed. She loved animals and art, so she and I shared many interests. Janice and I had developed a pattern in our work together—as we greeted each other and engaged in conversation, I would write down words or phrases on a blank page of her art journal. Her communication was limited due to dementia; her words were often confused, but intonation and facial expression helped me to understand her. I wrote her words down exactly as she spoke them in bold print, occasional profanity and all. She read the words back to me as the corners of her eyes crinkled into a delightful smile, perhaps amused by her own words or pleased at the acknowledgment me writing her words symbolized. She preferred watercolor and she would start making marks with paint or markers all around the edges of the written text or the collage image. Her marks were purposeful; she often paused to consider her progress and she chose her colors carefully. When finished, she would lean back in her chair and hold her book at arm's length, admiring her work. Her daughter arrived for regular visits at the end of art sessions, and Janice turned the pages of her art journal, showing her daughter each new mark and vocalizing more than she did otherwise. Janice often tried to give the book to her daughter, but her daughter always said, "No Mom, you keep it for now. I would love to have it when you are gone, but you are still working in it now." I promised both of them I would ensure the book would be safe and would get the book to Janice's daughter when the time was right.

Janice continued to work with me, both in open studio sessions and in individual art therapy. When I walked up to her, her eyes would brighten as she smiled, saying, "Oh! It is you!" She had come to associate me with good things—trips outside in the garden, animal visits, and time creating art. I worked with her for almost two years in individual and group art therapy. Her vocalizations became less frequent, but her attentiveness to her art process and interest in art never wavered. When I announced our clean-up warning each session, she regularly folded her arms across her chest and said, "It's not fair!" Her words expressed what she, her daughter, and I all felt—we wanted to linger in the space where we were all just artists, delaying the return to the new normal, where she had dementia and lived in on a locked floor of an assisted living.

When Janice died, her daughter and I sat down for an hour in the art studio together and looked through her art portfolio. It was one of the most intimate and touching goodbyes I have experienced with an older adult—and it came a month after her death. Her daughter had returned to sign some final paperwork and collect the last of her mother's belongings. We sat in Janice's spot in the studio and slowly went through her art journal page by page. I shared memories about Janice's process and her daughter traced over the spidery pencil lines with one finger. She read the words I wrote on the page aloud, much like her mother had, and I shared details about her gesture and intonation. My role with Janice was as a fellow artist as well as an archivist; writing Janice's words down preserved not just her quirky turns of phrase, but also her voice.

CHAPTER 4

OPEN STUDIO SETTING

Open studio art groups have many benefits for older adults. This chapter covers some suggested practices and materials as well as tips for inviting elders to participate and ways to encourage creativity in the setting. It covers best practices for space design and utilization, how to handle interpersonal issues in the open studio setting, and ways to introduce prompts without the session becoming an art instruction class.

Unfortunately, many of the situations art therapists encounter are set up in opposition to effective work with older adults. As a recent art therapy graduate, I did some contract work for various assisted living and skilled nursing care settings. My role was to arrive, do a project, and leave within the space of an hour. When I walked into the room at the scheduled time, I either encountered an empty room and had to compress our time for creating while people trickled in, or I encountered a restless group who had been assembled too early—neither situation got our creative process off on the right foot. I did what I could to create a welcoming, creative space, but sometimes the logistics precluded any opportunity for creative work. Looking back on it now, I would make some logistical changes if I were in the same situation again.

The qualities of the space are especially important for open studio settings, but not reliant upon having a beautiful art studio. Trays of natural items, interesting collage material, and images from art books or magazines can be set up as points of inspiration. It should be made clear that the intention is not necessarily still life or replication of the inspiring image. Simple things like proximity to water and easy storage solutions can work toward an environment of empowerment for the elders. If they are able to assist with things like washing brushes, they can feel more autonomous in the space. It may feel, especially for students or new professionals, like doing things for the older adults is caring and helpful, but it can be perceived as the therapist having a lack of trust or a lack of confidence in the older adult.

Particularly in assisted living or other care-providing settings, the participants are likely to need different amounts of assistance, have diverse physical needs, and have different comfort levels with art materials. Because of this reality, a space that can be changed and adapted in the moment works best. Rather than one large table or individual workspaces, I like to set up multiple smaller tables into an "L" or "T" shaped table; this table arrangement allows me to see everyone, gives the feeling of togetherness, and accommodates individual needs for space or distance from peers. If there are people working with particularly messy or disruptive materials, I will set up smaller workspaces as needed. If tables, rolling trays, and other adaptive seating options are available those are great to have; the art therapist can also adapt the space to individual needs in other ways, using books or boxes to prop up work areas. I like to have clipboards or art drawing boards available in case someone is unable to work at the available tables. I always endeavor to make the space work for people instead of letting the space dictate how people work. I learn a lot from the older adults about adaptation; many of them have developed innovative ways to adapt their environments with simple tools and modifications.

The open studio setting can become the type of group proposed by Cruikshank (2013) as an antidote to earlier life experiences:

> To be old and psychologically healthy in a society marked by destructive impulses requires great equilibrium and balance. In supportive groups, older women could perhaps come to regard moving slowly not as humiliation but as a chance to tap into the life force that is unnaturally suppressed by speed and fragmentation. (p. 7)

A studio space without pressure to create, and with subtle signals that it is a place to linger rather than produce, can meet this need. When they first enter the studio, they may feel pressure to produce or to finish something in each session. I encourage them to work on long-term projects as appropriate. I also use my ongoing projects as a way to model this behavior.

"Tell Me What to Paint"

One of the most frequent requests from older adults new to the studio or new to work with an art therapist is "tell me what to paint." This request reveals more than a creative block or artistic tentativeness: it reflects passivity and an overreliance on being performed to or done for. Passivity is common in older adults with dementia and has been studied in intergenerational art therapy groups (Stewart, 2004). Many care-providing settings perpetuate these common behavior patterns by filling calendars with performances or memorization-focused trivia. These activities are not designed with collaboration or interaction in mind.

Similar to the older adult asking for a step-by-step project, younger people may tell older adults what to paint or make attempts to intervene in the process. Art therapists should model an open, accepting, and creative approach, and gently ask the well-meaning younger person to allow the older adult to work on their own. I will sometimes accomplish this by talking directly to the elder, saying, "Sometimes we artists need to make messes or scribble a little before we figure out what we want to do," or "Sometimes I like to just hold the materials for a while before I start working." If the younger person persists in over-assisting, I will set a direct boundary.

Robert created a watercolor painting exemplifying his experience in the freedom of the open studio (Figure 4.1).

Figure 4.1 Robert created this watercolor painting spontaneously during an open studio session. He worked on it over the course of two hours. The words go in all different directions because he rotated the paper as he was working.

When I asked him to explain the piece, he pointed to the word "RULES." I asked what he thinks about rules and he surprised me, saying he likes them. I experienced him as a joker and had not expected this answer. He laughed and continued, "I like the rules because then you know when to violate them." He enjoyed painting with non-traditional tools like toothbrushes and sticks. He often painted at arm's distance or with his paper down on the floor beside his wheelchair. Near the end of this session, a nurse approached him, requesting he return to his room so she could change the dressing on a wound. As he moved his wheelchair back from the table, he looked at me, rolled his eyes, and stated, "You see? Rules!" I could hear him laughing down the hallway as he went to meet with the nurse. The freedom of the studio allowed him to respond to the medical care needs with a sense of humor and may have a reparative function for his sense of autonomy.

Painting from Her Belly

An art therapist working from an empowerment framework can undo some early biases against art established through poor instruction, familial priorities, or faulty internalized belief patterns. Anna's art experiences prior to entering the open studio squelched the budding artist within her; she described a teacher who was punitive and discouraged creativity. She often described this teacher with anger—someone who demanded compliance and perfection. Anna was very self-aware and able to identify old belief patterns when she was engaged in creative practice: "I spend too much time worrying, so I'm tired after painting! Instead, it should clear out my mind." She kept meticulous records of her artwork and made comparisons between pieces created at different times. She and I worked to explore more gestural approaches to mark-making. We also worked on repurposing experiments she was unhappy with; I encouraged her to cut the paper up for collages or try incorporating other materials. She came to describe her new approach to creating art as painting from the belly.

As she continued working in art therapy, she also connected the new approach to art as a way to feel more at peace with the aging process:

> I think there's a point when we get old where there's an acceptance of old age and also there's a point where we just say if you're a certain age, things just happen in your body and if you accept it, you make it easier on yourself and everybody else—don't complain and make a fuss!

When she started art therapy she had a great deal of anxiety about her husband's dementia and her own physical decline. She worried about exhausting the medical professionals she interacted with, bringing long lists of questions to appointments and worrying about small details. She was being proactive about her health, but the anxiety meant she never felt soothed or reassured; she could never ask enough questions or write down enough information. The process of making it easier on herself in her art helped her to make less of a "fuss" about her physical experience of aging. She continued to be proactive about her health and advocated for the needs of her husband through his time in hospice and in the last days of his life, and she did so with an increased sense of balance.

After five years of work together, Anna had become more comfortable with a wide range of materials, was far less anxious in her daily life, and was approaching being able to claim her creative identity: "Oh, I'm not an artist—I consider myself a painter who uses watercolors." She had artwork on display around the assisted living and set up a little art area in her room. Her enthusiasm for art was infectious; a peer commented on her excitement after listening to her describing her work: "A person who does art for the first time—they don't have a vision for the future, they need to see the joy you have in the simple shapes." Anna's joy was wonderful to be around and she brought infectious enthusiasm into the studio.

Release and Relax

Sylvia had complex trauma history and several additional mental health concerns. She had been in intensive therapy for many years, but was struggling to continue to pay for her weekly sessions with ever-increasing medical costs and care needs. She had wide-ranging interests in the arts, especially poetry and drawing. The woven bag slung over the back of her motorized wheelchair often contained several dog-eared books of poetry along with an apple, a notebook, and other essential items. She had a fierce political mind, laughed easily, and looked out for her fellow residents. Sylvia was conversant in many topics, yet she struggled socially in the assisted living setting because she expressed her history openly. Talking about trauma, depression, and anxiety alienated her from her peers.

On rare days when she was feeling calm and playful, Sylvia came to the studio laughing and would fill pages with humorous sketches of her cat. More often, Sylvia used time in the art studio as a way to sublimate the intensity of her emotional experiences. She would come through the studio door, make eye contact with me, and nod as she found an open spot at a table near the door. I learned her silent nod meant she was not yet ready to talk to anyone and I brought her paper and mark-making tools. She preferred charcoal or oil pastel, pressing hard to achieve richly pigmented images. She depicted scenes from her dreams or unresolved issues from her past. Sometimes she would want to discuss the image when it was complete, quietly bringing it over to me and telling me about the contents. Sometimes she would just turn the paper over and make eye contact again before leaving the room. She knew I would date her drawing and put it safely into her portfolio. Occasionally she would come back later in the day to talk. She never worked on images more than once; they were snapshots of her physical and emotional state. When she did make the choice to stay in the studio after drawing, she was able to talk with her peers without her distressing thoughts interrupting her ability to interact.

Sylvia was always able to tell the story of her images; the many years of therapy made her adept at describing her inner experiences. What was different with the art therapy was her ability to see evidence of pain or struggle on paper and to show the visual representation to others. She often wondered aloud why no one had ever encouraged her to draw her difficult experiences before. Occasionally she expressed frustration, but most of the time the communicative power of her images filled her with wonder and gratitude.

Her drawings were either simple, clear depictions of single emotions (Figure 4.2) or very complex. The small face in Figure 4.2 is surrounded by a field of black charcoal. It conveys the experience of grief—a darkness threatening to swallow the figure. In her darkest moments, this image was the way Sylvia showed up to the dining room table or in other common areas: no space for connecting to others and overwhelmed by darkness. In one of her complex images, she depicted each of her different worries and anxieties as snakes in a snake pit. She colored each snake with a different color; they all tangled together in knots at the center of the page. The subsequent week, she created a large amoeba-like figure on a page—black with spots the same colors as each of her snakes. She labeled the drawing "A Creature No One Could Love." She said each of her anxiety and worry snakes made a mark on her—things she could not get rid of that made her experience difficulty in social settings. After we discussed her art, seeing how distressed she was while looking at the two images, I asked her to create an image depicting something that could help with the snakes. She labeled a piece of paper with the words "Snake Pit" and then created a drawing using charcoal pencil (Figure 4.3).

Figure 4.2 Sylvia's image of grief. The ellipses on either side of the title appear almost like tears coming from the word.

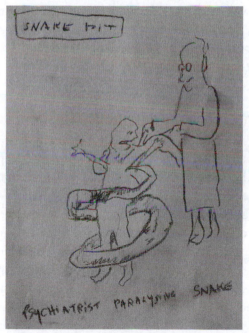

Figure 4.3 Sylvia's second drawing of the snake pit has only one snake and depicts a psychiatrist taming the snake.

In the drawing, she depicted herself as small and child-like. The most evident facial feature is a mouth open in a gasp of horror. The arms are small and appear like they would be ineffective against the snake, but unlike the grief drawing this figure does have arms. Behind and slightly above her, a male figure with a resemblance to Freud holds out his arm to paralyze the snake. She said the male figure represented her psychiatrist. She was worried about what she would do when she could no longer afford to see him. We continued to work together on building up her sense of self and her sense of resilience through her art.

She did not show her peers the complex images, but the more simple ones became an opening to authentic communication with others. She gradually began to incorporate some of her feelings into the humorous drawings of her cat. In one piece, a figure she identified as herself is nose to nose with her cat while a small demon with long claws approaches woman and cat from behind, about to interrupt their tender moment. When she showed it to another elder in the studio, the woman laughed, and then told Sylvia she knew the feeling. The two of them discussed different things the demon could represent and discovered they both struggled with anxiety and fears about affording their care as well as discomfort with needing to ask others for help. Being able to interact with her peers in the art studio enabled Sylvia to engage in prosocial behavior instead of becoming overwhelmed by her own emotional responses.

Difficult Interpersonal Dynamics

We could always hear Nancy coming before we saw her; with an irregular gait and jingling jewelry she seemed to stomp through the building with her cane and later her walker. When she entered the quiet studio, any previous sense of calm or quiet was shattered—particularly if someone was in the seat she claimed as her own. She would stand over the person and clear her throat loudly and then demand the person vacate her chair. Nancy was an artist—specifically basketry and weaving. When we first met, we got off on the wrong foot: the executive director at the time introduced me as her new teacher. I quickly replied that I hoped it would be the other way around, but the damage was done—it took almost a year to gain her trust. I had to reassure her I saw her as an artist first and not a student or patient.

Her behavior represents a pattern discussed in professional conferences and written about anecdotally, though not widely studied (Burling, 2018; Span, 2011). The behavior put into context is described as "social manipulation and exclusion…more to do with acquiring power, a feeling of control, at a point in life when older people can feel powerless" (Span, 2011, para. 11). Nancy's need to assert her power and sense of independence drove her to dominate the conversation in the studio. She came in and jumped from one topic or complaint to the next, often repeating the same sets of grievances from the prior week. For those who sat at the dining room table with Nancy, they might hear her complaints several times each day.

Nancy had a loud voice and very strong personality. Though I later came to understand her prejudice as fear about her own cognitive state, she could be cruel to people with cognitive decline. She would announce loudly that she did not want to look at or be near "those people." It seemed like she was fearful dementia could be transmitted through proximity. Interestingly, she was incredibly kind and protective toward peers with physical limitations or medical concerns; her closest friend in the studio was another artist in the end stages of fighting cancer. Nancy brought her special treats from the grocery store, a pillow for her chair, and always included her in conversation. She mourned her death for many months afterwards and often brought her up as we worked in the studio.

When Nancy no longer felt threatened by my presence we had a much better relationship, so long as her identity as the best artist in the community was upheld. My role in the studio with her was both artist's assistant and referee—maintaining an awareness of the ways Nancy's behavior affected her peers, strategic seating, and occasionally shifting the conversation. Her negative attitude could impact the whole studio. Conversely, her creativity and enthusiasm for learning was infectious. I assisted her in obtaining materials and learning new techniques; she and I worked together to learn a wire weaving technique, laughing as we struggled to master it and at the wild behavior of the long lengths of wire. I assisted her as she created an altered book about her life, finding images of the neighborhoods she lived in and collage materials specific to her travel all over the world. Nancy became very generous with praise and creative instruction as she felt more seen as an artist and leader. She shared her experiences with me and with her peers.

The Living Studio

When the studio setting is thriving, it operates as the hub of the community. Each time I have established a studio practice in an elder care community any initial skepticism about the viability of lengthy sessions or multiple art groups is wiped out as older adults arrive early, linger past the scheduled stop time, and request more open time to create. Even for those who do not consider themselves artists, the space becomes a desirable place to be. I overheard a resident telling a caregiver that she was planning to attend the studio session to be with the group: "She's such a nice person. I have no talent, but they're all such nice people that I like to go." Many older adults sought out the community we created because of the laughter and vibrancy emanating from the groups.

CHAPTER 5

CONNECTING BEYOND DIAGNOSES

This chapter covers ways to use art therapy as inclusive, community-building practice. Older adults in congregate living situations are often grouped by their level of care need or diagnoses, not necessarily by their interests or passions. Interactions as creative individuals help them to learn about and connect to each other. These interactions can also be used to address some of the stigma around stroke symptoms, dementia, and Parkinson's—stigma that can lead to bullying and exclusion. I have seen a formerly judgmental, standoffish elder completely reverse his opinion about a resident with dementia after seeing her art (Figure 5.1).

Figure 5.1 This simple cat drawing was a connection point between the resident who created it and her peers. She drew it on a scrap of tracing paper and, because she liked it so much, we mounted it on white paper and immediately framed it.

The woman who created this simple cat struggled to make social connections because of symptoms of dementia and speech difficulty after cancer treatment. The art became a way for her to introduce herself and to demonstrate her sense of humor, love of animals, and creative talent. Her peers praised the simplicity of this image and her ability to capture the essential nature of a cat. The art process can also stimulate open and often humorous conversations about the aging process; one woman, after describing herself as "forgetful: totally full of forgetting" had the whole group laughing as she described what a bowl full of forgetting would look like. When I asked her what a bowl full of forgetting would taste like, she wrinkled her nose and said, "It would taste horrible!" The images and conversations created in art therapy can be building blocks for increasing community cohesion.

Interacting with older adults presents many clinical and diagnostic opportunities—I have observed early signs of dementia in elders' artwork prior to any other symptoms. One resident in assisted living, who was not exhibiting any other functional impairment, suddenly ceased to be able to use visual symbols. She had previously created many faces and human figure images, but one day while creating a face, she was unable to draw features and instead wrote the word for each feature in the location it belonged within a head shape. I have also seen older adults make images exhibiting signs of a stroke or other issues with physical health. The art therapist needs to maintain his or her knowledge about the diseases and disorders of later life and how they might manifest in the art products, but the intention of this philosophy of art therapy with older adults suggests that a focus on empowerment and connection is essential.

One of the most important things for the art therapist to do in these types of situations is to tend to the qualities of the elders. Ensuring they are treated, discussed, and connected to as artists enables them to transcend any diagnoses and to connect with each other and their larger community as people. Art materials and creative output are less important than the authentic human connections that happen during the art process. Processes in the art studio have also uncovered talents and histories among the elders who were no longer able to speak their history aloud. While facilitating a weaving group with some residents with very advanced dementia, I handed a skein of yarn to a woman with limited mobility and no ability to verbalize. As soon as the yarn was in her hands, she seemed to have a new level of energy in her body: she sat up tall in her wheelchair and lifted her arms away from her lap. I held the loom closer to her, and she started weaving: over, under, over, under across the row. Later, I spoke with her family and learned she had done many forms of fiber art over her lifetime. She and I wove together many times over the next few months, spending peaceful afternoons in the sunny area near a window. My experience of her during those times was so different than in other settings: she made direct and continuous eye contact, regularly reached out for my hand or for a new color of yarn, and exhibited more physical strength and ability than I otherwise observed. Her story is a reminder to us to continue to offer and attempt work with people, even if it seems like they are unable or uninterested—the right material makes all the difference.

Dignifying Their Words

As with the work with Janice in Chapter 3, writing down the words of people with dementia or people whose voices may not be heard or understood establishes a sense of equity among group members beyond any symptoms or diagnoses. It communicates to the older adults that their words are heard and they matter. The images they create in art therapy can also function as a substitute for or supplement to verbal communication (Abraham, 2005; Ehresman, 2014). In a conversation about memory loss, two residents shared their experiences. As they talked, I wrote down their words of wisdom and read them back. One of the residents said, "In short, we are defining ourselves, our characteristics, based on the quality of our conversations." She described feeling like no one had patience for her anymore, because she asked the same questions repeatedly. After I read her statement aloud the group nodded in agreement and told her she had made a smart observation. She reacted with a big smile, patted my hand, and told me we would now be friends because I took her seriously. She took the paper with her quotation and added a human figure and her name in big letters across the top of the page. Seeing her words written on paper invited her into the group and helped her have the confidence to create an image. Her creation initiated a conversation with another resident at the table—someone who presented as more cognitively stable and less impacted by symptoms of dementia. She held her peer's image at arm's length and talked about how she related to it, and to the need to create: "I forget more if I hold onto the negative qualities of our conversations—it acts as a block against what I want to do right now. I need to use more art and just live live live!" In that moment, diagnosis did not matter—the two women connected with a shared experience.

Occasionally, I create a piece during the studio session using the residents' words as a prompt. One older adult told me about a time she grew frustrated with a peer at her lunch table who was asking every few minutes about where her kids were. In an attempt to soothe or silence her she exclaimed, "You know in your heart they love you! Stop asking!" The resident described how heartbroken she felt when her peer responded quietly, "I can't hear my heart." Her words brought tears to both our eyes—those simple words so clearly explain the experience of someone with dementia. Using the woman's statement as a prompt, I created two pages in my art journal, one using paper cut outs and a second page created by making a rubbing of the first page. The resulting image had intense metaphoric resonance, like the echo or ghost of memories just beyond perception. Later, I used this same paper collagraph technique in a group setting, using a word from each participant to form a single composition. The process of creating the rubbing was like repeating or chanting the word and the tactile, repetitive experience of creating images in this way is an effective approach when working with a group of people with stratified physical abilities and cognitive status. It brings purpose to perseverative, self-soothing movements by recording motion with art materials.

This way of creating work can also be connected to the work of the contemporary artist Jesse Houlding; he uses repetitive and kinetic processes to create his work. He described the importance of repetition to his art in an interview:

> I have been thinking a lot about how repetition operates in an artistic practice; from thinking about repetition as a self-soothing gesture to the ways a repeated mark accumulates and takes on a new meaning by the sheer magnitude of the mark making. I think this is in part why I am drawn to the kinetic work, I like the hypnotic quality of the movement but at the same time am interested in the way it changes over time. (McKenna & Grattan, 2012, para. 6)

The qualities Houlding described can be present in collagraph images created by older adults as well. If appropriate, sharing examples of Houlding's creative processes helps to give meaning to their work.

Collagraph word project

Materials

- Paper for collagraph plate (try experimenting with different weights and textures of paper).

- Paper for rubbing (lighter-weight paper works best for this part of the project).

- Scissors.

- Glue sticks or other adhesive.

- Wax crayons with wrappers removed or other pigment sticks.

Process

Invite participants to choose a word or group of words to work with.

If working as a large group, the art therapist can cut letters out or utilize letter stickers. As an alternative option, participants can utilize shapes to create compositions.

After the word composition plate is created, participants can choose their rubbing paper and a color to create their rubbing with.

Each participant can create their own rubbing, or if using a large sheet of paper, participants can choose different colors and create a group composition.

Once rubbings are complete, invite the group members to add to their images. They can use a wide variety of materials to create their own expression using the group composition as a starting point.

If appropriate, invite participants to share their images and their processes for creating. Engage group members in identifying similarities and differences among the different images created from the same plate.

The Smallest Marks Tell a Story

Elenore was an accomplished artist—an expressive oil painter whose pieces sold well enough for her to support her family. When I met her, she was in the very late stages of dementia and had been in the skilled nursing setting for many years. She often moaned and drooled, behaviors that distressed more cognitively aware peers. In efforts to soothe the milieu, nurses parked Elenore's wheelchair, along with another woman with similar symptoms, in front of the nursing station. As the dementia progressed, her distress seemed to increase; one of the activity assistants brought her to the studio one day and announced that Elenore was an artist who wanted to come meet the other artists. This woman, a long-time employee and someone with more knowledge through experience than any of us with advanced degrees, was exactly right: Elenore needed to be in the studio.

I sat down on a low stool next to her chair and put my hand on hers. I welcomed her into the studio and invited her to come back anytime. It became our weekly ritual. The activity assistant brought her to the studio each week and they would stay as long as Elenore seemed content. One day, I decided to try an experiment. I took a small paintbrush and placed it gently in the palm of Elenore's hand. Her eyelids fluttered but did not open. "It's a paintbrush, Elenore," I said softly. Her fingers rolled the brush and shifted her grip to that of an artist ready to paint. I looked at my coworker and exchanged an amazed glance—neither of us expected such a strong reaction. I brought a small piece of paper and some watercolor over to where we were sitting. Narrating my movements aloud, I guided the brush to the water and then the paint. Then I supported the underside of her wrist and held the paper right at the tip of the brush: "Okay Elenore, you can paint now." The room was so quiet we could practically hear the bristles on the paper as she began moving her hand, making short, purposeful brushstrokes. The motions she made were very different from her typical movement—they did not seem to be a result of tremors or other involuntary gestures. We also noticed her shoulders melt down away from her ears as her whole body relaxed. Most significantly, when comparing the brushstrokes she made on paper that day with her large painting in the living room, we noticed the quality of the marks were nearly identical—like they had been reproduced at 50 percent of the size of the original work. Bringing Elenore into the studio restored her dignity and may have brought increased purpose to her last months of life. Her time in the art studio seemed to soothe anxiety and reduce the distress she had been communicating in her body language.

Vision Not Required

When I first met Rebecca, she was polite but reserved. She came to the skilled nursing program from the hospital and was overwhelmed from the transition and by all the people she was meeting. Later in the week, after all the assessment and admission paperwork was over, I went back to talk. Her family told me she "used to be an artist" and I wanted to understand what the past tense meant to her. Family members often apply past tense to pursuits and interests of older adults, leaving them in a strange situation where their only identities in the current moment are related to age or diagnosis. I told Rebecca her family mentioned she liked art; she smiled and shook her head slowly. She described a lifelong love for art and literature; she authored several books and was an accomplished watercolor painter. She especially loved painting flowers and the landscapes of northern California where she lived for most of her adult life. When she moved into an assisted living, she shifted to painting still life compositions and the view out of her bedroom window into the rose garden. Because of the paintings she created and displayed around the assisted living, she became known as the artist in her community. She created many paintings of the view from her window with different lighting and weather conditions, not unlike Monet's haystack series (Metropolitan Museum of Art, n.d.). Rebecca told me that her vision had been declining for years due to macular degeneration. She noticed daily tasks steadily becoming more difficult. When she went to see her ophthalmologist, he bluntly pronounced, "You're blind. You'll have to give up being an artist." She went home, packed up her paints, and never touched them again. Her story brought tears to my eyes, imagining what it must have felt like to have her passion abruptly shut down by a misguided medical provider.

In addition to macular degeneration, Rebecca was experiencing significant hearing loss. She wore headphones with an amplifier around her neck to improve her hearing, but it only helped a small amount. Research has identified macular degeneration and other age-related vision loss as a major barrier to continued participation in leisure activities and hobbies, with negative impacts on quality of life (Berger, 2012). Older adults with dual sensory impairment are at risk for depression, isolation, and decreased quality of life (Berry, Mascia, & Steinman, 2004; Heine & Browning, 2004; Khil, Wellmann, & Berger, 2015; Roets-Merken, Zuidema, Vernooij-Dassen, & Kempen, 2014; Saunders & Echt, 2007). I was concerned about Rebecca's psychosocial wellbeing as well as her artistic identity. Hearing loss made it very difficult for her to interact with her peers and low vision made it hard for her to see and interpret social signals.

I gently asked Rebecca what she was able to see. She described a "ghost-like" shadow world, similar to descriptions of life with macular degeneration I had heard from other older adults. Gently guiding the conversation back to an area of strength, I asked Rebecca about her writing projects and what she was currently working on. After hearing about her plans to write a postscript to her memoir, I asked her if she would like to paint again. She hesitated at first and began asking tentative questions about how we could do it. I put a piece of textured paper under her fingertips and asked if the sensation in her fingers was strong. "Yes!" she said, "I feel that!" I asked her to tell me what sorts of things she would like to paint. I explained that I could create a textured canvas for her, with hot glue lines she could read with her fingers. I also encouraged her to come into the art studio to visit with everyone if she did not feel like painting: "You are an artist and you should be in the studio with us!" I intentionally used the present tense, signaling to her that I viewed her as an artist even though she had not painted in several years. Rebecca was excited and had me inform the nurses that she wanted to come to the session in the studio the next day.

When she came to the studio the first time, I had an area prepared for her. I set out a large, blank sheet of watercolor paper along with a simple still life image of a vase with a few flowers created with the raised glue lines as we discussed. I made the forms simple with different line weights and line quality: curvy lines for the vase and spiked flower petals and leaves. Instead of a small watercolor palette, I brought several plastic plates with watercolor paints separated by color family. After describing the layout of her workspace, I invited Rebecca to choose between getting the feel of the brushes again on a large piece of blank paper or trying out the new technique. She responded with a laugh that she might be out of practice and would like to "use the brush like a musician warming up before a performance." She made big, exuberant brushstrokes, splattering paint across the table. Her smile stretched from ear to ear and she was painting so vigorously the table shook. The other participants in the studio that day looked on with curiosity for a minute or two but then returned to their own work. After a few more minutes of her warm-up, Rebecca paused, took a deep breath, and looked at me expectantly: she was ready. When Rebecca and I began working on her still life, the questions started:

How are you able to tell where you are painting?

Are you really unable to see?

How do you know what colors to use?

Noticing she had not heard the queries from her peers, I repeated the questions to Rebecca one by one so she could hear them. Her voice, clear and strong, answered each question with dignity. She explained that she was feeling her way across the page with her fingers and her mind. She described the way the brush felt like an old friend and that her memory of the different colors assisted her in making choices. She laughed and told everyone that she did not know if the end result looked any good to our eyes, but in her mind, it was a beautiful vase of flowers like the ones she used to pick.

She returned the studio every week for the remainder of her life. Her experiences in the studio and with her peers increased her self-confidence. This self-confidence extended beyond her time in the studio; we observed her making more requests, advocating for herself with her medical providers, and, most significantly, calling herself an artist again. In the postscript to her memoir, she described reclaiming her artist identity.

Working with What Is

Valerie, like many of the older adults in the studio, came to art later in her life. Prior to my arrival at the assisted living where she lived, she attended weekly art classes facilitated by an art teacher. Valerie had a diagnosis of Parkinson's disease; her symptoms manifested primarily through stiffness in her legs, slowed gait, a slight tremor, and what she described as hallucinations when listening to music. She said it was like the notes went into her ears and became all jumbled and discordant in her brain. She used to enjoy attending musical performances and could no longer do so because of the disorienting symptoms. Parkinson's disease is a dopamine deficiency secondary to nerve cell deterioration (Funk & Wagnalls New World Encyclopedia, 2014). Art therapy is recommended for older adults with Parkinson's disease (Waller, 2002), but it can be difficult for them to participate in traditional art-making, depending on the severity of their symptoms. Waller described the frequent comorbidity of depression and despair with many progressive illnesses: "There are few who can tolerate a relentless progressive loss of their faculties, an inability to feel part of the world, such an assault on their person" (p. 5). Depression and anxiety are common for people with Parkinson's (Perepezko, Pontone, & Minton, 2018); the symptoms can be exacerbated by the disease's impact on communication, mobility, and quality of life. Involvement in creative processes, particularly when appropriately adapted to the person's level of functioning (Leverenz et al., 2013), and focused on the person's ability rather than disability, can assist the person with Parkinson's disease in feeling more connected to the world.

The first time Valerie attended an art therapy session in the studio, she expected it would be a continuation of the projects facilitated by the art teacher. The teacher had been providing pen outlines for older adults to add color to. While the art teacher was tending to qualities of the space, including providing inspirational images and some varied materials, she had inadvertently encouraged a culture of helplessness in the studio. In a study comparing coloring activities to open studio sessions facilitated by an art therapist, Kaimal, Mensinger, Drass, and Dieterich-Hartwell (2017) found that while coloring pre-made images has some benefits to stress reduction, open studio sessions facilitated by an art therapist demonstrate better outcomes in self-efficacy, creative agency, and positive affect. Though their findings were stronger for the younger participants in the study, that finding could be due to the short length of time of the study; given older adults' need for more processing time and differences in emotional expression (Kerchner et al., 2012; Mather, 2006), they might need more sessions to achieve similar results. Anecdotally, I have found that to be the case with older adults I interact with like Valerie, who are transitioning from provided coloring images to more free expression in art therapy. At first, Valerie struggled to find the confidence to make her own compositions. But over time, her confidence increased and she began venturing outside into the garden before coming to the studio in order to pick flowers to create her own arrangements to draw from (Figure 5.2).

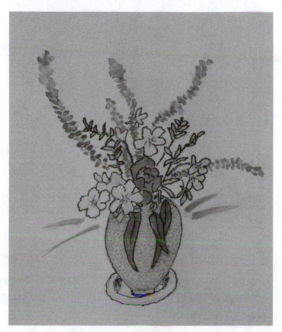

Figure 5.2 Valerie's ink and watercolor painting of a bouquet she picked in the garden. Here, she was replicating the type of image previously provided for her by using thick ink outlines and adding color afterwards.

As the Parkinson's disease progressed, it became more difficult for her to create paintings of flowers she felt satisfied with. I encouraged her to explore different kinds of mark-making with the paintbrush—things that would not rely on fine motor control or be as impacted by the tremor in her hand. Valerie grew very excited as she explored the wide vocabulary of marks she could make with different brushes. She created vibrant patterns and mandala-like circular compositions. She and I also worked together to develop a set of cards using her floral paintings and new expressive patterns. She set up a table in the living room each month to sell cards. She used the money to satisfy her sweet tooth and to purchase new art materials. When holding the paintbrush became difficult for her to do for long periods of time, we began creating collaborative collagraph prints. Valerie, like many older adults I interact with, had been saving assortments of objects in her room and would occasionally divest herself of these collections by bringing them to the studio (Partridge, 2016a). She liked the shape of the dental flossers she used and thought they might make an interesting pattern (Figure 5.3).

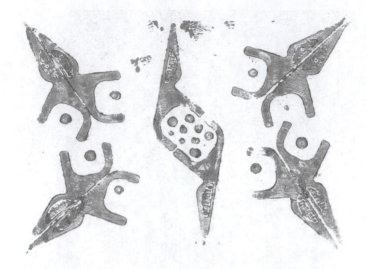

Figure 5.3 Collagraph print created with acrylic paint on paper. We used a sponge brush to apply the paint because Valerie found the brayer too difficult to control.

After she arranged the plastic flossers in a pattern she was satisfied with, I assisted her in gluing the flossers to a stiff piece of cardboard. We experimented with creating both frottage rubbings as well as collagraph prints from her plates. Valerie's progression from passive coloring to creative abstraction and use of found objects illustrates her progression through creative empowerment.

Living in the After

Father Thomas started coming to the art studio accidentally. One afternoon, he followed someone else into the room, sat down across from me and held out his hands in a gesture as if to say, "Now what?" I handed him a piece of paper and a pencil, which he took. After looking to the left and right at his peers quietly working on their projects, he started drawing. Much to everyone's amazement, including his own, he began drawing well-proportioned and often very expressive human figures, mostly young men in heavy jackets. He described them by telling stories about his own life, which he often ended by saying, "but that was before…" His voice would trail off as he gestured to the room around him and then to his own body. Occasionally he would elaborate by verbally describing his physical state or tapping his forehead and shaking his head from side to side. He said he did not know what to do with himself since retiring from the priesthood. Growing up in a very religious community, he spent his entire life preparing for and carrying out his role and was not sure about his identity beyond his role as a priest. Retirement can be a difficult transition time for many, for clergy it involves not only a vocational but a spiritual transition; the clergy member experiences "upheaval as he moves from the role of leader-participant to observer-participant" (Ladd, Merluzzi, & Cooper, 2006, p. 84). Interaction in medical or care-providing settings can compound feelings of disempowerment or identity loss. Father Thomas needed to explore and discover who he was in the current moment. As he continued attending the studio sessions, we all discovered part of who he was after: an artist and a storyteller. He also discovered his sense of humor. In one of his first paintings, he drew and then added acrylic paint to a portrait. He described this person as chest-deep in water, but did not elaborate much about how the person came to be that way (Figure 5.4).

Figure 5.4 Portrait of a man chest-deep in water. Father Thomas used a gradation of blue acrylic to depict the deepening water.

His experience of creative self-discovery in the years after retirement was not unique among his peers. Over the years, many elders came to the studio out of curiosity or peer-prompting and found they enjoyed painting, collage, or other creative pursuits. They found new identities as artists in time after retirement.

CHAPTER 6

PROJECTS WITH PURPOSE

Art therapy directives and independent art pursuits are a way to connect older adults to the larger community. This chapter covers art therapy in response to new, community-specific events, and issues related to social justice. It includes case examples from both assisted living and dementia care programs, and suggestions for ways to establish partnerships with community groups, youth, and social movements.

A sense of purpose in life has many implications for physical and psychological health. In a study of time perspective and sense of wellbeing, researchers discussed the importance of being able to plan for and anticipate future events (Desmyter & De Raedt, 2012). These future events cannot be simply ways to fill time—they need to be connected to a sense of personal or community purpose and have meaning. Projects with purpose can translate into feelings of personal purpose. A sense of purpose is one of the outcome goals of many programmatic interventions and part of a wellbeing scale for people with dementia (Bradford Dementia Group, 2008). The creative arts therapies have been described as an effective treatment for the emotional and psychological impacts of mild cognitive impairment and dementia because the "therapeutic stimulation through art therapy and music provides an affective antidote to the isolation and other debilitating effects" (Galbraith et al., 2008, p. 267). Creative practice allows older adults to reimagine who they are in the world and establish a new sense of purpose; one of Stephenson's (2014) participants described herself as "a source of history, a vessel for providing legacy" (p. 8), a role she connected to through aging and being creative.

Reactions to the News

Common practice in care settings for people with dementia encourages sheltering or shielding older adults from potentially distressing news. The rationale seems to be about avoiding upsetting the older adults or causing needless agitation. The reality of care settings, however, means that if it is an event with any amount of news coverage, people with early to middle stages of dementia are likely to overhear and understand the content and implication of the news. Emotional communication has been explored as an adaptive response to verbal communication difficulties (van Dulmen, Smits, & Eide, 2017). Even those with more advanced dementia, depending on the type, may maintain close to their full emotional capacity or physiological responses to emotional stimuli (Sturm et al., 2011). Older adults with dementia are aware of the social and emotional environments around them; opportunities to express and identify emotions are supportive of their social connectedness (Bober, McLellan, McBee, & Westreich, 2002). These findings in the literature do not support shielding elders from difficult news events. Attempting to conceal bad or distressing news puts care partners in a far worse situation—not only is the older adult upset about the news, he or she may also be upset that the news was concealed, severing the relationship and creating mistrust. Because care partners often assist with intimate care tasks, a sense of trust is essential. Assisting someone with bathing, eating, or using the restroom requires some level of trust between those involved—when there is not trust, the person with dementia may express distress through anxious or agitated behavior or complete refusal. Anything that puts the relationship at risk should be avoided.

Boston is strong

In the past several decades, the increased coverage of local and international tragedies has captured the attention of us all. Older adults, even those with dementia, need outlets for expressing their responses. When the Boston Marathon bombing happened (Eligon & Cooper, 2013), Robert, a resident in our memory care setting, was devastated. He had spent most of his adult life in Boston, lapsed into the accent whenever he talked about his life there, and encouraged everyone he met to go to Boston to visit and bring back postcards. On the day of the bombing the news station was not on in the memory care area; he overhead the coverage when returning to memory care from a trip down to the assisted living building to watch a performance. Nurses told me he stopped in his tracks and refused to move until the coverage went to commercial break. He talked about it all through dinner and did not sleep. The care staff attempted to distract him and did not answer any of his requests for more details about the bombing. I came to work the day after the event and he ran up to me, asking me if I had heard about the bombing, asking if he could go visit, and asking if I had any more information: "They won't let me watch the news! They said it is too upsetting! This is my home! I need to know what is happening in Boston!" Robert was normally the clown of the memory care building, easy-going and a leader among his peers. He assisted with setting the tables for meals and groups, welcomed anyone who came to visit memory care, and generally charmed everyone he met. His hair and clothing were always meticulously tended to. On this morning however, he was still in his nightshirt and sweatpants, his hair was uncombed, and he looked frantic in his eyes. He had seen the news and could not unsee it. I do not write about this example to shame the care partners: they were doing the best they could at the time in trying to tend to the needs of the entire milieu. But Robert needed an outlet. He needed to feel some connection to the moment and to his former home.

In our art group that morning, I suggested Robert create a message to send to Boston: "What would you want the citizens of Boston to know? What do you want them to feel? If you were there right now, what would you want someone to say to you?" He grabbed a handful of supplies and got right to work to create his image (Figure 6.1).

He slowly traced around the edges of a stencil. Then he started filling it in with black watercolor on the right side: "That's the dark smoke," he explained. Robert carefully rinsed his brush and switched to a golden yellow color and filled the other half of the shape. Satisfied with his work, he requested a ruler and created a thick blue border around the whole sheet of paper. With a marker, he titled his piece and signed his name at the bottom—his name took up almost as much room as the title. Once complete, as was his usual practice, he held it up and asked the rest of us in the group, "What do you think?" I asked him where he would like to see that message in Boston and he replied that he hoped it would be in every window and every mind in Boston. He grew quiet and after a short silence told us that he was not too worried, because "the people of Boston are so strong." I suggested that he, as a long-time Bostonian, was strong too. He smiled, batted his eyes, and made his customary exclamation: "Wooo! I AM strong, darling!" Even with his nightshirt on and sleepless eyes, the charmer we all knew was back at the table. He asked for some tape in order to post the image on his door. He continued to refer to the strength of Boston over the next few days, but his distress was greatly diminished after the group. He was not asking for the news to be switched on and he seemed to have returned to his baseline. What I learned from this experience was the importance of a safe environment to explore feelings in memory care settings. Dealing with the Boston bombing directly assisted Robert in reframing his encounter with a scary news story to a story of strength and resilience.

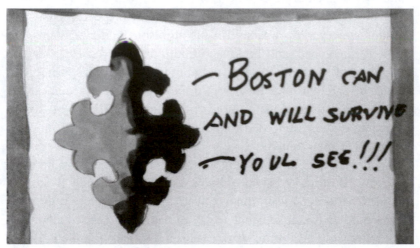

Figure 6.1 Watercolor and colored pencil response to Boston Marathon bombing [detail].

Subsequent terror attacks, natural disasters, and political unrest have necessitated a wide range of art therapy interventions with the older adults. In assisted living, we sometimes used the newspaper headlines as a jumping-off point. Elders have created protest signs and tribute art, occasionally collaborating with family or staff to deliver their work to the site of a tragedy or to a community gathering. Impulses to shield or protect need to be examined for infantilizing or paternalistic reasoning. Part of empowering older adults is approaching them as whole people capable of dealing with the full spectrum of human emotion.

Representation at protests and public memorials

When the political discourse focused on immigration, older adults in memory care created messages of love and inclusion. Although not all residents in memory care were able to attend, several assisted living residents held the signs at a peace vigil we attended at an immigration detention center; it was powerful to witness the elders holding their peers' messages and participating in a community expression of solidarity. At one point, the leader asked if anyone would like to address the group—one of the elders spoke up and explained who made the signs and where we were from. She not only made older adults visible, but also those who were unable to be present.

After a tragic fire at an artist loft a few blocks from one of our communities, the residents were full of questions; they wanted to talk about the young people who died, they wanted to talk about fire safety, and they wanted to create some kind of response to the loss of young lives. Some of what they were worried about was the similarity they saw—a big building with many people living inside and a failed evacuation. They worried about how our big building could be evacuated and about getting stuck or left behind. We could not avoid addressing it—the smoke was thick in the air and the helicopters had been hovering over the area for several days.

We started by driving by the burned building a few days after the fire. The fences on all sides of the block were covered in flowers, balloons, and messages of love. The van was silent as we approached and I heard someone suck in a big gulp of air as we approached. When we gathered in the art studio on the following day, several residents expressed interest in contributing to the community message of support. We talked about the need for artists to support and protect each other and I asked them what kinds of support and protection they needed. They worked for several hours on cards, which I took to the site that afternoon. I photographed their cards in among the other messages to share with them later.

The responses from the older adults both to the peace vigil and the tragic fire had significant meaning in the moment of creating and then a larger impact when brought out into the community. Joining in community rituals is an important part of human life (Dissanayake, 1995b), and making space for older adults and enabling their participation signals to the elders that they have a role in their community.

Community response directive
Materials

- Some of the materials may be dictated by the type of event or situation. For example, responding to natural disasters like fires or floods can be addressed through metaphoric use of materials like watercolor, spray-pigment, or charcoal.

- Copies of newspaper articles, especially headlines, about the tragedy.

- Cards or cardstock.

- Scissors.

- Glue or glue sticks.

- Simple mark-making tools.

Process

Start the group by facilitating an open discussion about the event or situation. Use this time to clarify any misunderstanding and to orient the group to the situation. This can be a helpful time to address any fears or anxieties the group members are concerned about.

Invite group members to create a card or message to those impacted by the event. If possible, identify one or two possible recipients or locations to send the cards—this might be to a shelter or aid group providing services at the location. If sending the cards is not possible, identify a location in the building where the group meets for a temporary display of the responses.

If the messages are on display in the building, include blank paper and simple materials so viewers can add their input and reactions as well.

Difficult Family News

I witnessed families using many different strategies to deal with difficult news stories and sad personal situations in my time in memory care settings. One family decided they did not want to tell their mother about her husband's death. She was in agony every day—pacing the halls, rattling the doorknobs, and asking everyone who came into the building, "Have you seen my husband?" Other repeated questions included "Do you have a car? Can you take me to see my husband?" and "Did my husband's doctor call?" Though she was in the middle stages of dementia and had not seen her husband in several years, she remembered he had been in the hospital. His hospitalization precipitated her move into memory care. The faint memory of him in the hospital bed increased her anxiety about locating him. As the dementia progressed, her fixation on and anxiety about her husband increased. It prevented her from engaging in groups for any meaningful length of time: anytime she heard the door or a voice outside the room, she left the room to ask her battery of questions. It felt inhumane to conceal the information from her, but her family had expressed their wishes and continued to affirm their belief it was in her best interest to keep the information from her.

In contrast, another family practiced gentle, repeated reality checks with their mother. Anytime their mother asked where her husband was, her daughters held her hands, looked right into her eyes and said, "Daddy died many years ago. We all love him and miss him. He was a great man, wasn't he?" As their mother's eyes filled with tears, they would suggest making a card for him or looking at photos. One of the daughters told me that before they began using this approach, their mother would tell them that she was worried she had not seen him because he was cheating on her—concerned he had gone off with another woman. Her worry caused sleeplessness and depression. Their new approach caused tears, but it maintained the sense of love and familial connection. It also approached the older adult as an emotionally competent and resilient adult, able to work with and process strong emotions.

Art therapists can be of great assistance in these situations—art directives designed to honor those who died or creating memorial spaces to visit in memory care can help to reduce perseverative behavior and require less emotional labor from family members. When these directives are used in a family group session, it can assist family in learning new ways to interact with their loved ones and can provide the entire care team with new information about the person with dementia in order to provide the best possible person-directed care.

Family memorial directive

This directive benefits from coordinating with family members to have them bring copies of photos or other important mementos for inclusion in the memorial. It can also be helpful to find out important facts about the person and have relevant collage images cut and ready to use. For example, if the person was a doctor, have an image of medical symbols or tools.

Materials

- Colored paper.

- Small boxes to create shadow boxes.

- Canvas.

- Photos and collage materials specific to the person.

- Photo corners.

- Basic art supplies.

Process

Invite the family to share stories as they work together on creating a memorial image. It can be on canvas or on a piece of art paper to fit into a frame or shadow box. Encourage the older adult with dementia to lead the creative decisions—the family should assist with applying glue, but the elder should make the decisions. For older adults with more advanced dementia it may be necessary to assist the family in paying attention to things like the direction of the elder's gaze or other subtle cues indicating interest in one element over another.

If the person is able to verbalize, invite them to describe their piece and the person they are honoring. If they are non-verbal, allow time for the person to sit with the image, holding it or touching it if possible. Family and art therapist should quietly serve as witnesses.

When the elder has finished responding, either verbally or non-verbally, invite family members to share a few memories of the person being honored and what the image means to them.

Once the piece is completed and all in attendance have responded, ask the older adult where he or she would like it to be displayed. If possible, be ready to hang it immediately.

Intergenerational Projects

Creating opportunities for older adults to work with younger people is about so much more than community service. In our interactions with youth, the residents become leaders, story-keepers, and mentors. These projects also provide rich opportunities for younger people to grow and also shift their opinions about older adults. An art student described what she learned from her interactions with older adults in assisted living: "Sometimes I think I'm not doing anything, but then I realize things are just slower—and it makes me value short conversations." She described herself as someone with an excellent memory and that interactions with people with mild cognitive impairment and dementia taught her other ways to interact and engage. She also described the impact she had on older adults—helping them reconnect with a sense of purpose: "I am changing their perspectives of who they are; I help them remember that they are useful." Connecting with different schools provides mutually beneficial opportunities.

Mutual support

I had a wonderful opportunity to work with a family for several years. The daughter was just transitioning from childhood to adolescence. She and one or both of her parents joined me for an art group once a week over the course of several years as volunteer assistants. They also attended community events like holiday parties and performances. As we worked with the elders, I witnessed this young woman grow and change; she became more vocal and confident in our groups. The older adults with dementia provided boosts to her self-esteem at a critical point in her life—they accepted her just as she was each week and vice-versa.

In an effort to explore the impact of intergenerational work, I invited this volunteer and an art student intern to create images about their experiences with older adults. The three of us created mixed-media paintings and wrote statements describing how the world sees older adults, how we see older adults, and our hope for a future without ageism. The adolescent volunteer's statement about her piece demonstrates the empowering, deeply nuanced view of older adults she developed through her work with them:

The world sees older adults as broken-down people that can no longer take care of themselves. They see them as very black and white. I see older adults not as the handicapped, dull people many others see them as but rather as individuals with personalities. Softer than younger adults—like a variety of pastels. I also recognize that some elders do have trouble walking, but many others are active and able to take care of themselves. I'd like older adults to be viewed less as broken-down people but more as themselves. I suppose looking beyond their physical shape and focusing on their personality. Treating them as you would any other adult.

She used an architectural template labeled "human figure: geriatric" to create different silhouettes representing older adults on a vibrant background, and filled some with black and white acrylic while others were filled in with the pastel colors she wrote about in her statement (Figure 6.2).

Figure 6.2 Adolescent volunteer's depiction of how the world views older adults and how she wishes it could be. Acrylic, ink, and vintage shelf-paper on panel.

The artwork we created and our statements are up in the lobby area of our support center offices as a reminder about both the power of intergenerational work and the communicative properties of art.

Art about our ages

As part of our work to address ageism in our communities, we initiated a call for art that became an exhibition of work from artists from infancy to over 100. Participants were asked to create an image on a square foot canvas or paper representing something good about being their current age. We used the format of a square foot show as an equalizer: everyone's voices got the same amount of space. As part of their submission, participants were also invited to consider and answer the following questions:

- How do you define or describe your age?

- Do you feel connected or similar to those in your age group or generation?

- What does the world say about your current age?

- What is good about being the age you are right now?

We encouraged people from all different settings to participate. Additionally, I facilitated several studio sessions in offices, museums, and care settings. In one of the museum sessions, three generations of one family participated; as they worked, they shared their images and their experiences with each other. In one of the assisted living settings, a grandfather used his image as an opportunity to encourage his granddaughter to travel—something he wished he had taken more time to do. The studio sessions brought people of all ages to the same table and often stimulated intergenerational conversations about ageism, misperceptions, and unexpected joy in each decade of life.

The 168 submissions for the initial show spanned a wide range of media and included photography, weaving, fiber art, collage, and painting. The written and verbal responses were overwhelmingly positive; participants at all ages were able to identify many different benefits to each age. The question about how the world perceives people their age elicited similar responses from the adolescent and older adult participants. Both groups expressed feeling dismissed or misunderstood by other generations. Their words described ageist encounters on either side of adulthood:

> Society says that 16 year olds don't know what they're doing. They're sort of blundering through life aimlessly, trying to figure life out, doing stupid things in the meantime. (Age 16)

> We are not going to make it out, we are failures. (Age 16)

> Some respect and cherish; others are dismissive as useless or even a problem. (Age 76)

> It says we are limited in what we can do after a certain age. By the way, they are wrong. (Age 84)

The resulting body of work was exhibited at the offices of a university's dementia research center, a large elder care conference, and the headquarters of an advocacy group. For the exhibit at the conference, we had several long, narrow shelves for the art, which I rearranged throughout the conference. Attendees were able to add their square foot pieces to the body of work, so the show evolved over the four days of the conference. This project invited people of all ages to engage as experts in their own experiences. For the older adult participants, the opportunity to exhibit their art and showcase their ideas in several large forums was exciting.

Because of the public nature of this show, the large settings where it was exhibited, and the breaks in chain of possession, the pieces created for the show were made outside the art therapy context. I facilitated work groups specifically to create work for the show. Some of the older adults I worked with took their pieces home to work on. As the show traveled, I provided updates to the older adults—though they could not travel to Chicago and Washington, DC they followed the project from their communities.

CHAPTER 7

Mural Projects

Murals have an important place in human life. Walking around cities, one is likely to encounter many types of murals or large-scale outdoor images. In contrast, walking around inside an elder care community, the walls are often plain or decorated with faded floral prints. Some of these prints languish on the walls for decades. If the walls were filled with murals, imagine how much more dynamic and vibrant the environment could be. Murals often occupy public space and are used to communicate to those who encounter them (Coffey, 2012; Low, 1902; Theisen, 2010). Murals have been part of political uprising across the world (Coffey, 2012; Goalwin, 2013; Latorre, 2008; Rolston, 2003) as well as peace and rebalancing processes (Anderson & Conlon, 2013; Berberian, 2003). Murals can impact the people who create them as well as the people who view them:

> Growing directly out of the hopes, dreams, and desires of the surrounding population, community-driven public art gives a voice to those who inspire it and provides a breath to all those who pass it as it speaks from the streets. (Baca, 2009, p. 29)

In art therapy settings, murals can serve a similar function. Art therapists use murals to explore family and group dynamics (Kaimal & Gerber, 2007; Landgarten, 1987), and support treatment goals (Argue, Bennett, & Gussak, 2009; Liebmann, 1986; Trzaska, 2012). Many of the goals and objectives of mural art are relevant in older adult settings and could be utilized as a form of empowerment for older adults.

This chapter covers several different mural projects with groups of older adults with dementia and murals created in collaboration with undergraduate art students. It also discusses mural art as an accessible art appreciation venue through "scenic drives" to view murals. This chapter uses case examples and a research project to introduce ways to use murals as empowerment and sites of connection in art therapy.

Murals as Camouflage or Stimulus for Engagement

The reason behind using murals in elder care settings influences both the content and process of the murals. Several examples in the literature discuss the use of murals or other environmental changes to disguise exit doors or otherwise contain or soothe older adults with dementia (Cohen-Mansfield, Thein, Dakheel-Ali, & Marx, 2010; Kincaid & Peacock, 2003). Similar practices include fake bus stops or other fake waiting zones in memory care settings (Miller, n.d.; Verity, 2007). These practices, while well intentioned, are potentially coercive. Though best practices have shifted away from lying to people with dementia, camouflage murals are a form of non-verbal deception. Coercive use of murals is particularly out of sync with the social and historical place of murals as community empowerment and messengers of social justice (Rossetto, 2012). Mural work with older adults can instead be used to create large, dynamic images and to support social connection (Woywood & Davenport, 2013). The scale and visual impact of mural work transforms the environment.

Welcome In

Instead of camouflaging the interior of a door to keep residents with dementia inside, I worked with residents in a locked memory care program to create a mural installed at the doorway on the outside to invite visitors into the space. This project required navigating several different interests—the needs and timeline of the renovation, the aesthetic interests of the leadership, the desired theme for the mural, and the abilities and interests of the older adults. I did not regularly work with this group of residents, so I had to design something we could count on completing within the existing timeline for the doorway renovation that would also be therapeutically appropriate and enjoyable for the residents.

We worked on a sheet of wood veneer cut to the size of the area where it would be installed. I provided high-quality materials in a wide range of colors in order to invite the residents to participate. I brought acrylic paint and brushes as well as acrylic paint pens. Street and mural artists are driving new development such as low-odor and low-toxicity spray paint, water-based paint pens, and other vibrant art tools. These tools are more expensive than the materials typically provided for people with dementia but they should be considered. They are often refillable and available in a wide range of sizes making them ideal for adaptive art therapy. I brought acrylic paint pens with large barrel diameter; these tools are easier for people with limited mobility or hands impacted by arthritis to hold. As the work evolved, we also incorporated some collage and natural materials. I planned the project to be completed at the end of two group sessions. In our first group, we focused on making large marks, experimenting with the different brushes, foam pattern stamps, and textured papers. As we created, we talked about their interests. One woman gave a vivid description of a horse. I asked her to tell me all about it and as she talked, I painted a simple red horse with a long flowing mane on the canvas right across from her. She had her eyes closed while talking and when she opened her eyes and saw what had appeared on the canvas she gasped aloud, "My horse!" I invited her to outline the shape in the color of her choosing and to add additional details. Using a pink acrylic marker, she made the mane and tail even longer and encircled the horse several times. When the staff came to look in on our progress, she excitedly showed them her red horse.

Another resident described the planes he flew and worked on during World War II; I made a note to myself to find images of his planes for the subsequent group. At the end of our session, we admired our work and talked about plans for the subsequent group. Though lunchtime was approaching, the participants lingered, not ready for our session to end.

Several family members of the residents were present and wanted to participate when I arrived for the second group the next week. I brought real horse hair to attach to our red horse and some images of the plane described by the resident in the first group. Similar to our first session, I had acrylic paint, brushes, and paint markers. When I brought out our work from the prior week, the family members were amazed at the size of the piece. Size is one of the impactful elements of mural work with older adults—especially those with dementia. So much of their life is restricted and condensed—the ability to make big, bold marks or take up a whole wall with their ideas signals to the world that they should not be pushed aside or overlooked. The family members' responses and the pride on the faces of the elders were exactly what I hoped for. We spent two hours painting, residents and family coming and going, filling the panel with color. When it was done, one resident asked me where it was going to go. I explained that it was going to be permanently installed in the building at the entrance to their community. He smiled from ear to ear and asked if he could watch them build it in. I told him I would appreciate him being there if he was able to, in order to make sure the construction crew hung it right side up. He laughed and I passed his request along to the memory care director after we cleaned up for the day.

The piece was installed on time and it is absolutely beautiful. It is under glass right alongside the door. Instead of the door to memory care being dominated by the access buzzer and signs about closing the door behind visitors after entering, it is filled with color, ideas, and memories. The door does not communicate restriction and disease but rather life and community.

One unforeseen issue that came up a few months after the installation was a family member who wanted her mother's portion of the mural after her mom died. All the residents' responsible parties had signed releases for creating this group piece, but the daughter's grief led her to ignore the reality of the form she signed, the cost of tearing the entire doorway apart, and the potential impact to the rest of the community. The chaplain in the community was able to spend a long time talking with her and helped her agree the mural should not be cut apart or removed. We created a canvas print for her with a close-up photo of the part her mother had worked on. As with any group projects, a piece of mural art's eventual display and life after the creative process concludes can be complicated. Art therapists need to work with staff and leadership to ensure all participants understand the eventual display of large group projects and that any necessary consent and release forms are signed.

What If We Could?

The end of one of the hallways on a memory care floor was a collection point for chairs, lost sweaters, and other objects of dubious origin. The wall had a small, knee-height door into a storage crawl space and two windows up at ceiling height but no view to the outside. It was beige and depressing. The hallway on the other end of the floor led to a beautiful window seat with a view down into the gardens. The contrast was striking and seemed unfair to the older adults with rooms on the dark side of the floor.

One day, I asked a few residents if they would like to discuss the idea of painting a big mural on the wall. They were skeptical at first, but with playful energy I invited them to imagine we already had permission and all the materials we would need. At first, they thought we were just discussing a solid paint color; "blue is nice," one woman suggested. As they came to understand we were talking about painting a big picture, their voices grew more animated. One woman, in a matter-of-fact voice, told the group we should "paint California, since that is where we are." Observing the group's nods of agreement in response to her statement, I asked what parts of California they wanted to include and we talked about their favorite cities and landmarks. Most of the participants were lifelong residents of the county and felt a strong connection between their cities of residence and their identities. We also talked about nature—all the beautiful plants and animals they had seen in their lives. After a lively discussion, we settled on a theme of California native plants and animals.

For our next session, I gathered with a group of five older adults around my computer. Using keyword image searches, we looked at photographs of different options to include in our mural. When we found a plant, animal, or landscape photograph they liked, I imported it into a layer in an image processing program. I put each element on a different layer so we could make adjustments to the composition later. Once we had several animals, several landscapes, and several types of plant life, we began working with the different layers and designed our mural. I set up the file to be the dimensions of the wall space, so we were working within the proper shape. They made all the decisions about which things to include, how big each element should be, and where each element should be in the mural. After our design session, I printed out our image and we solicited feedback from other residents and family members. The family members of one long-term resident who was in the very last stages of dementia informed us that her favorite place in the state was up in the redwood forests, so we added redwoods to the side of the mural closest to her room at their suggestion. The final design featured a California quail in the center, surrounded by lupine, poppies, butterflies, ladybugs, redwood trees, and a mountain lion with her cub. Using native plants and animals created an opportunity for the older adults with dementia to be teachers; they identified and explained the different animals and plants to the care staff, many of them immigrants from other countries. Asking questions and identifying similar natural elements from their countries of origin became a way for the care partners to establish stronger rapport with the residents.

When the design was approved by the older adults and the leadership gave us permission to begin, I projected the design onto the wall. Once the pencil outlines were complete, I invited the residents to come join me. As we walked down the hallway, they asked repeatedly where we were going—it was not an area of the building we spent much time in. As they arrived, they understood we were about to do something different and special. I set up a semi-circle of chairs facing the wall and I had a printout of the design ready for each person. Off to one side, a table displayed all the paint colors we would be using. I poured out some bright blue paint and then asked one of the residents who was able to walk unassisted to add the first color to our wall. He stood up and rolled a wide stripe of blue across the wall. Then he turned around, gave everyone a big smile, and took a bow. For months afterwards, he told people with pride that he was the first person to paint "our mural." From an empowerment perspective, it was essential to invite one of the residents to apply the first paint on the wall and to continue inviting their input and participation throughout the project.

The process of this mural was different from smaller group murals I had done—because of the size of the wall, the physical ability of the older adults involved, and the need to paint on ladders, I invited a friend with mural-painting experience to come volunteer with me. She frequently brought her young daughter to paint with us, adding an intergenerational element to our work. When possible, the older adults in memory care painted the areas near the handrail; we arranged chairs near the wall and put drop cloth down underneath them. Throughout the process, no matter who was painting, we stayed faithful to the design the older adults created. Some of the older adults who participated had not engaged in any other art processes with me. One resident promised me at the very beginning that she would do "one brushstroke." I invited her to paint each time she walked by, but she would shake her head, say the work was beautiful, and then resume pacing. One day she agreed and I handed her my paintbrush without pause or hesitation. She was a tall woman and she stood right next to me and painted one burnt sienna brushstroke on a redwood tree. Surprisingly, after she handed the brush back, she sat down and watched for 20 minutes as I continued working on the redwood section. Then she stood up, reached for the brush, and said, "I did not fill it in the way you did." She painted for about five minutes: long, steady brushstrokes up the trunk of the tree. When she was done, she handed the brush back and went on her way. An hour later, I overheard her telling a family member that she had been painting the mural that afternoon.

During the painting process, older adults from all levels of care enjoyed watching the mural evolve. When I looked down from the ladder, I saw their alert, curious faces looking back at me. We had conversations about the different sections of the mural and discussed color choices and painting technique. Though they were not often actively painting, they rarely dozed off or looked away while the mural painting was going on; they watched closely and shared their observations. They looked at the printed pictures of our original design and the additional source material. Their most frequent questions were about color mixing and sequencing—they liked to ask what was going to happen next and then inform peers who arrived later. The elders narrated the mural process.

Beyond being a way to address a cosmetic problem in the interior design, it became a way to engage the residents. The dark end of the hallway was no longer an unused space collecting lost objects. We used it as a wall-sized game of "I spy" and a prompt for storytelling. It served as the vibrant backdrop for a miniature restaurant, which helped one woman sit down for a full meal for the first time in months. It was a way for mother and daughter to reminisce about a favorite animal and share family history and memories with the care partners. From start to finish, this big mural was about empowering those living with dementia—putting their words and actions on display and showing the whole community that a dementia diagnosis does not mean an end to expression and innovation.

Intergenerational Mural Projects

As part of an ongoing partnership with an art college, we had the opportunity to work with a community art course. Through their programs for community and public art, this course paired an entire class for a semester with us as the community partner. The class was designed to teach both skills and strategies in group projects, and ethical social engagement with community populations. Prior to working with us, previous semesters paired students with a cultural heritage center, the food bank, and homeless adults with mental illnesses. Each semester, students learned from the community partners and collaborated on murals. We requested the students work with the theme of holistic wellness. The professor and I walked through the building and decided the best location for the murals: the walls of the large dining room in assisted living. Pairs of students were assigned to design and complete 4 × 9-foot murals on panels. The finished murals were to be installed once they were complete. The students were also required to attend several brainstorming meetings at the assisted living and to complete 15 hours of volunteer time with the community. To welcome them into our community, we hosted them for several lunch gatherings. They used this time to research, asking the older adults about their lives and getting input into their ideas and practices to support wellness. In addition to their work with the older adults, I facilitated a discussion with them about the domains of wellness (Foster, Galjour, & Spengel, 2015; Pizzi, 2001; Strout et al., 2016) and the importance of a holistic approach to wellness for older adults. Each student had time to share their own experiences with older adults; they completed our art-based evaluation on the first day of class and again during their final. We use this evaluation for all our intergenerational programming (Appendix B). In the case of the mural project, the professor and I used the students' responses to guide our reflective discussion after the project was complete.

Large, public projects like this are not immune to criticism (Senie & Webster, 1998). Several residents loudly voiced their disapproval of the project from the beginning. Despite repeated invitations to come and discuss their concerns with the students, they did not attend. Their displeasure was part of a larger complaint about the organization, and had little to do with the mural project itself. One of the elders who did participate silenced a peer when she complained again after the work was installed: "You had plenty of opportunities to come talk about what you like and don't like. You chose not to come, so now you don't get to complain!" Her words demonstrate the important role these types of projects play—she felt like a stakeholder in the project and defended it against a negative peer.

At the celebration party for the mural project, one student shared the meaning of the project for her: "Being an art student is lonely and dark." She went on to describe the strange relationship to art assignments that lose their meaning after the semester ends as compared to the murals, which will live and evolve in the space. She was right: the murals continue to be a source of dialogue and interest. The residents tell me their opinions about the different pieces and how they change over time. Interestingly, the critical voices have been less vocal since the initial uproar—once the work was installed and the older adults who participated voiced their positive experiences with the project, their complaints stopped.

Working with these students was such a pleasure and seeing the impact the older adults had on their art was even more touching. When I visited their art studio at the college to see the paintings in progress, I could immediately tell which residents each group spent time with—their stories and personalities showed up in the work. The students really listened to the interests and experiences of the older adults. They were generous both with their time and with their creative talents. The permanent installation of the murals has transformed the dining room and is a very visible example of the community's interest in maintaining intergenerational connection for the older adults who live there.

Amplified Voices Mural

The Amplified Voices study investigated communication in the elder care context (Partridge, 2016b). Study participants created individual images and participated in interviews about their lived experience of intergenerational communication. As part of the data analysis, older adult co-researchers designed a mural about communication in care-providing communities for elders. The older adults directed the process for planning, painting, and exhibiting the mural. During a discussion of the history of mural art, they requested a drive around the neighborhood to see more mural art. The mural process took 15 sessions, involving discussion, the mural drive, and painting. While working with the individual art-based data, the older adult co-researchers made several observations about the collection of images. They noticed the frequency of the use of dots to represent spoken communication, the relative simplicity of the images, and the importance of even subtle references to gesture. They concluded that all forms of communication needed to be illustrated in their mural design with an emphasis on the importance of touch. One participant said posture was the least important because it can be misinterpreted: "Your posture won't tell the whole story." This participant went on to connect age and posture as areas where people make assumptions and generalizations. As a way to present the elder participation data in a more holistic way in the dissertation, three participants were described in detail. Their interaction with the mural process is summarized in the following vignettes: Gloria, Betty, and Alvin.

The advocate

Gloria attended the drive to see community murals and attended some of the planning and discussion groups. She tended to hold back, observing her peers or making quiet statements. One of her contributions to the discussion about best practices in communication was to emphasize the importance of touch—both human contact and the importance for people to be able to touch the mural itself while it was in progress; she was one of the participants who advocated for painting the mural flat on a table instead of onto the wall in order to enable a greater number of people to participate.

Gloria did not participate in the individual interview and art-making. She said she did not want her responses to impact the outcome. It is possible she used her advocate role as a way to distinguish herself from the other assisted living residents. Prior to retiring, Gloria had been a care coordinator in the building. Her new identity as a resident and sometimes as a care recipient created difficult-to-navigate role confusion. She continues to refer to the message in the mural two years after the completion as a way to understand her peers as well as a way to track changes in her own communication.

Making herself heard

Betty was one of the people who were able to participate thanks to Gloria's advocacy. She was in a wheelchair and unable to lift her arm past mid-chest height, but she could reach to paint the mural since it was flat on a table. She had also participated in the individual image-making and interview; in her interview she spent a long time talking about the ageism she experienced throughout her later life. She attended most of the mural groups and also assisted on the day I installed the mural on the wall. She spoke loudly in the group setting, and often spoke over other people; it did not seem to be intentional. She apologized several times when she became aware that she interrupted someone. The volume and speed of her speech alienated her from her peers; other participants expressed to the researcher that they felt they could not make themselves heard.

Betty was not well liked by some of her peers, which became apparent in the group process. One assisted living resident stood up from her chair and looked down at Betty sitting in her wheelchair when defending some of the group's choices about the mural composition. As she said in her semi-structured interview, she has a high level of intelligence and self-awareness, so she was aware of the dynamic. As the group discussed how much of a smile to have on the two large figures, Betty discussed what she was experiencing in the group through the metaphor of the figures in the mural:

> Some people smile a lot, some people don't. My voice carries; some people think I'm yelling all the time. I don't know whether that's an asset or not. The problem is, it's okay for a man to do that, but it's not okay for a woman. When a woman starts to climb up the ladder, she is forced to become masculine. It's a male-dominated culture. If a woman wants to assert herself, she has to make herself stand out. Be heard. But how do you put that in a picture?

She made many sociocultural observations throughout the mural process, often referencing issues of sexism and ageism. During the final mural discussion group, she talked about the importance of considering the audience for the mural in the same way one considers audience for spoken language.

During the first day of mural painting, Betty expressed feeling worried about her shaking hands, but was able to paint a large area of the background. She expressed feelings of accomplishment at the end of the session. In another mural painting session, she said she had come to watch, but she did add her handprint to the border area, laughing about the feel of the paint on her hand and encouraging others to try it. As she watched the painting, she made observations about the image and about the topic of inquiry. She was a vital member of the mural groups and elder researcher team. Her spoken contributions and the dynamic she introduced into the groups brought up important aspects of communication.

The collaborator

Alvin was an established artist in the community and a leader during the mural discussion groups. He was very vocal in the groups, but never dismissed or talked over other people's ideas. When looking at the individual research images, he responded most to the body language he observed. He arranged images in sequences and described how the images could be part of a larger story, one set of figures leading to the next. When we began designing the mural, he prefaced each suggestion he made with a caveat that others were free to follow his suggestion or not. He said sometimes he had an idea and it "might not be the best idea, but then someone else builds on it and it goes from there." He described the collaborative process of creating the mural like a tennis match, where people look back and forth between different ideas in the search for the right one.

Alvin was hospitalized and died prior to the mural being completed, but the group chose to incorporate many of his ideas in the final design. The last mural group he attended, he was in a wheelchair. He was an active participant in the group, but he arrived late because he did not want to ask someone for help getting from his room up on the sixth floor; he slowly wheeled himself from his room to the elevator and through the ground floor where the group occurred. His devotion to the project demonstrated the impact of this type of project—he attended and participated despite the pain he was experiencing and the hardship involved in getting to the groups. Many of the other participants spoke about the importance of the mural design having originated with his idea. The mural was discussed during his funeral service; it became part of the story of his life in the community.

Murals in our neighborhood drive

Seven assisted living residents participated in a drive around the neighborhood to view murals. Using a map of murals in the surrounding area, I planned a route to see some different forms of mural art—murals created by schools, murals created by community groups, and graffiti murals. As we drove, we discovered additional murals, which we stopped to discuss. The elders tended to notice the little details in the murals: handprints, small design elements, repeated colors and patterns. They often talked about the tone of a mural, especially if the mural had a clear message it was communicating. They made observations about the colors used and speculated about the story being told in each image. We discussed the aesthetic and narrative efficacy of different compositions. Though the older adults enjoyed looking at the more complex, storytelling murals, they agreed that the compositions with one central image were most effective in communicating the intended message.

Driving around in the neighborhood enabled the participants to see art and imagery interwoven into their community. We saw murals on the sides of schools, businesses, and houses. We encountered many murals that seemed to be communicating community values and teaching about local history. The enclosed space of the van not only allowed us to cover a lot of ground and see more murals, it was also a safe environment for them to ask questions and voice controversial opinions. I was pleased to hear them asking nuanced questions about the role of street and graffiti art, and wondering aloud how to create messages that are both important and well received by the future audiences. One participant commented that she enjoyed hearing the different opinions: "One person would say one thing about what they saw in the mural and I was thinking the exact opposite...and they're both right!" This type of trip can be a way to see art, connect with community, and engage in discussion about the role of art in human life.

The mural lives on

A few months after it was complete, Betty told me she stopped to look at the mural every day and that she was interested to observe how well the different colors worked together. She explained how involved she felt in the entire process: "We didn't just watch this, we were part of it." Other participants continue to gesture to the mural as an example of inclusion and their role in the world; when new volunteers or projects come to the building, the residents make sure they see and hear about our research as part of their introduction. In summary of the process, one participant stated, "We get knowledge, we put it into action and do something with it. It helps us, it helps the group, and then look what came out of it all."

CHAPTER 8

ART ON THE WALL

This chapter discusses display, exhibition, and other ways to celebrate the work of older adults with a focus on the way these practices support connection and empowerment. It covers several different types of exhibition, addresses issues around confidentiality, discusses the ethics of art display, elders as curators, and reclaiming the walls as a form of empowerment and autonomy.

Depending on the setting and the specific confidentiality practices and rules, displaying work can serve as part of an empowering art therapy practice. Art therapists, researchers, and community artists have involved different populations in the public display of work as an opportunity for witnessing and empowerment (Clover, 2011; Lu & Yuen, 2012; Yeo & Bolton, 2008, 2013). Art therapists need to be very clear about the ethical guidelines for display of older adults' artwork. Reviewing the ethics documents from professional associations and licensing boards is a start. One also needs to observe all the guidance for confidentiality relevant to the setting, including protecting medical confidentiality. All that said, the powerful message communicated in the act of framing a painting or setting a sculpture on a pedestal should not be ruled out because of "unduly limiting" (Moon, 2016, p. 157) definitions of art therapy: the art therapist's role in many older adult care settings is less about providing clinical mental health treatment and more about being in community.

Transition from Craftsman to Artist

Alvin came into assisted living with a history of building and creating ornate birdhouses—objects designed, created, and placed in the environment with a predetermined purpose. Since he no longer had access to a woodshop, he started painting—first religious images, then birds, and then landscapes. His early work was focused on creating with a specific desired function or outcome for the art. His process of selecting and replicating images was very methodical as was his use of materials. As he grew more confident in his work, he began to experiment with larger formats and experimental mixed media. As described in the previous chapter, Alvin played an important role in our research mural. In work with Alvin, it became important for me to serve as both a studio assistant and a source of inspiration and information.

As we established a rapport, he and I developed a pattern in the studio sessions. We began each session with a joke from him and a new way to work with materials or point of inspiration from me. Periodically, I would suggest he try working larger or with a new medium. Occasionally, we switched roles. Our reciprocal relationship in the studio generated a sense of freedom, both for Alvin and for other residents in the studio; we demonstrated we could be creative without taking ourselves too seriously. When I introduced Alvin to the use of table salt, wax resist, and plastic wrap techniques with watercolor, his sense of experimentation and artistic bravery grew. He developed a sense of joy and exploration in the art process; his pieces no longer needed to serve a functional purpose but could instead be about the process of creating them and then enjoying them on the wall. He spent the first half of each studio session engaging in free exploration with the materials and then moved on to whatever more representational piece he was working on. The exploratory practices informed his more representational art; he incorporated the salt technique into acrylic washes in order to achieve the texture he wanted in a field of red poppies he painted. We hung this piece—his final large painting—on a wall in the family room near the lobby of the building.

Once his large painting was in a frame on the wall, he seemed to unceremoniously move on to the next project. At first, I thought he had returned to his previous way of working. This is where understanding the entire space is important and the art therapist who is not connected with the whole community may miss important details; Alvin had not moved on. One of the chaplains informed me she observed him visiting his painting each day on his way down the hallway to Mass. It seemed to give him great satisfaction to see his piece on the wall, and he continued to spend time in relationship to it as it hung in the community.

When Alvin died, his trustee donated all his work, including some birdhouses, to the community. Several older adults worked with me to select pieces and hang the exhibit. We created a memorial gallery on the floor where Alvin lived for many years. Seeing all his work exhibited on one wall, we could clearly trace his trajectory as an artist and creative person. His early functional objects and more illustrative style gradually evolved to incorporate creative techniques and deeper personal meaning. The exhibition of his work brought his role as a creative space-maker alive and ensured the memory of him would continue to inspire our groups.

Exhibition of the Undiscussed

Anna, as discussed in Chapter 4, did not have much confidence as an artist when we first met. As we got to know each other, I learned more about her history. Anna and her family had been taken from their home during World War II and placed in the Japanese American prison camps. The first time we discussed it, she told me she never used the term "internment camp" because that was not strong enough to describe her experience: "It was a prison. It was cold, it was gray, it was a prison." For several years, she told me bits and pieces of her story. It was not until I worked with her to frame a few of her unrelated images that she told me she had some drawings of the prison camp she would like to hang up. As she was reflecting on her life, she became aware that she was the only one of her family members who could still break the silence about their experiences. She wondered aloud whether sharing her thoughts and feelings about the prison camps and rebuilding a life afterwards might bring her greater peace. She also expressed regret and sadness that her mother and siblings would not have the same opportunity.

We returned to the idea over several months, and she decided that she did want to include the images as part of a permanent gallery in the community. She chose several charcoal drawings of the camp that depicted areas she had strong memories about. She also decided to include several of her more recent art pieces as a way to represent her growth.

While showing her work to a new volunteer, she described the impact it had to see her work on display: "Do you know she is the first person to put my work in a frame or hang it on the wall? No one ever did that for me before!" Hanging this work up allowed her to show her growth and tell her story. It was part of Anna's process of empowerment in later life.

A Star For All The People

For several months, I spent long stretches of the day with the residents in a memory care setting; we did some discussion groups and some movement, but spent the majority of our time engaged in group art projects. One piece, which the residents went on to title "A Star For All The People," exemplifies the qualities of empowerment-focused art therapy with older adults in several different ways.

I brought a large piece of canvas up to the memory care floor one day and asked the residents if they would like to try painting on canvas instead of working on smaller pieces of paper. We talked about the blank and boring walls in the room and their desire to make the space more beautiful. When they expressed interest in working together on a large group art piece, we taped the canvas down to the table with masking tape. We also used the tape to create patterns on the canvas. Our first session of work on this project involved painting large areas with different colors and marks. As we painted, we discussed our associations with the colors. One woman, who usually declined to participate, was so excited about finding a tube of paint in her favorite shade of lavender, she agreed to paint—something she had not done in previous interactions with me. She told us the color reminded her of her mother: "She wears this color all the time, and so do I!"

The next week, we unrolled our canvas. I reviewed our process from the prior session and we talked about which wall they wanted to hang the piece on when it was complete. We had not yet filled the center of the composition. I asked them what should go in the middle and one woman replied that "all the people" needed to go in the center. I had pre-cut magazine photos of people and asked her to work together with a peer to select which people we should include. When they made their selections, we used matte medium to adhere the collage to the canvas and continued to add lines and color around the edges. As a way to represent everyone in the room, I traced each person's hands onto the outside of the canvas. I made this a regular practice. Though the groups were supposed to be separated by level of care need and progression of the dementia, the lived reality of care settings often means art therapists and other group providers serve a group of people with drastically different levels of physical, cognitive, and emotional needs. Rather than cause conflict with the care providers or isolating those with limited ability to physically or verbally contribute, the art therapist can involve these older adults with tactile art processes and include their gestures and vocalizations in the rest of the group conversation. Tracing the hands of residents onto our large piece helped the more active residents connect with the others in the room. The residents who were painting filled the hand shapes in with different colors. The woman who loved lavender made her hand a light lavender color outlined in purple. As a final touch, we added a star above the human figures. When I asked them to title the work, they decided to call it "A Star For All The People." Their title seemed to acknowledge all the people present in the room as well as the diversity of the care community.

We drafted an internal press release to distribute inside the building, inviting residents, staff, and families to come see their new creation. It included an image of the work, some quotations from the older adults about the process of creating it, and an invitation to come see it in person. I gave copies of the press release to each participant and encouraged them to show it to their friends and family. One day, I overheard the resident who painted the lavender hand telling a staff member that she always knew which hand was hers, not because of the color, but because she was the only one who used her left hand on the canvas. Her memory for this small detail, despite her dementia, was fascinating to the care team; it helped them see her differently. The piece became a focal point of many groups in the room—the residents used it as an example to illustrate different ideas they discussed.

Several months later, the piece was taken down in order to repaint the walls. I was not present the day it was removed, and I did not regularly facilitate groups in that area any longer, but one day I went up to say hello and one of the original participants grabbed my hand and exclaimed, "I have been waiting for you! They took our piece down! Where is it? Where is it?" Her response demonstrates the importance of this image, not just to her, but as part of the community. I communicated her distress to the leadership team; it helped them understand the importance of the images we created and the art is back up as part of the resident art gallery. Our time together was about so much more than a painting for the wall; it was about connections as individual people with entire life histories.

A Final Chance for Creative Engagement

"My family never accepted me as an artist; they never knew me that way." Previously a self-described loud and rowdy New Yorker, Olivia's voice had slowed and softened since she went into hospice care but it still communicated her power and sense of self. Olivia was a mixed-media and found object sculptor; she often reflected with joy on her years of hoisting her small body up and into dumpsters to search for materials. She and I connected over our love for the wealth of art material available on the streets of New York. Now however, her tiny frame was curled up in her bed, hair in wild curls around her on the pillow. Her eyes still had fire though, and she croaked out her desire to have one last art show. I visited her at least once a day and we talked about her life, her art, and her desire to show her work. In all the time we spent together in her room or out in the gardens, we never created any physical work. We did reflect on images of her art and planned out her final exhibit. Interacting with her as a fellow artist was the important part.

One of the hallways of the ground floor had two inset wall niches; it was an old building and these spaces used to enclose drinking fountains. Now empty of any plumbing and painted the same neutral tone as the rest of the walls, they made excellent areas for art displays. Olivia's love for found objects and installation made these wall niches the perfect space for her art. She and I spent several hours looking through boxes of her small hanging sculptures and photographs of her larger work, looking for pieces that would lend themselves to the space of the niche. Her small pieces were jewelry-like, incorporating fiber, metal, and various found detritus from her life. In work with her, I felt pressure for us to complete our work and to have her show—I worried we would run out of time. I gradually learned it did not matter whether we installed the show: our work together and the conversations we had brought back her sense of agency and creative identity. Navigating the process of requesting her family get her work out of storage and proposing art installations in the empty niches brought Olivia the artist into assisted living.

We did end up completing our review of her work and installing her pieces in the week before she died. She and I worked for a whole morning to get all the pieces hung and the chaplain came by to take a picture of the two of us in front of her niche. After we completed our work, we went out into the garden to bask in the sun and reflect on her life. She died a few days later. In some of our last conversations, she told me how peaceful she felt to know her work had a permanent home and would not be cast away as trash after she died.

Elder Curators

If displaying work on the living space or studio walls is not possible, art therapists should consider ways the older adults can curate the space. Involve them in choosing framed prints or in designing displays, possibly including objects or collections from their own rooms. One elder in an independent living community was the head curator of our coffee nook. The nook area contained a buffet with coffee service and an empty china cupboard with lights and glass doors. It was designed to display objects, but needed a curator. She and I worked together to install monthly displays, both from her extensive collection of objects and from staff, family, and other residents. Sometimes she chose a theme and invited people to bring items related to that theme. Other times the inspiration came from a peer's artwork; she would select things to coordinate with the color or imagery. We also did a yearly memorial to deceased friends, family, and community members and holiday-themed shows for Valentine's Day, Easter, and Christmas. She took her role as head curator very seriously and arrived each installation day with her own tools. She kept notes about each exhibit and treated the space with as much importance as a gallery or museum exhibit. When asked, she gave "docent-led" tours of the exhibit for residents and visitors. This project gave her a sense of purpose and established her as a leader in our community.

What Goes in a Frame?

One of the most pernicious and strange things I have observed in older adult care settings is the lack of attention to what is hung on the walls. The framed images and other décor rarely demonstrate any consideration for low vision and dementia let alone the interests of the older adults in the space. Occasionally, the work seems to be in stark contrast to the lives and realities of the people who see it. Other times, the work on the wall is only slightly better than a blank wall. In contrast, well-chosen framed images offer opportunity for connection and conversation.

When asked to provide guidance to interior designers in our communities, I recommend images connected to the surrounding area; local libraries or historical societies can be excellent resources for these images. If choosing from stock images, I recommend images featuring clear subject matter, preferably humans or animals engaged in an activity. These types of images help to inspire storytelling. They can also be used as orientation or memory prompts; images related to dining outside the dining room can help residents with dementia find their way to the right room for their meal. We utilized written prompts under framed images in a memory care community. It helped give purpose to residents' pacing behaviors; staff could stop residents as they walked and interact by asking some of the prompt questions and writing the residents' response on the provided dry-erase surface. Abstract and non-representational images can work as well; I am always inspired by the stories older adults will tell about non-representational images. If time permits, I encourage discussion groups with the older adults, involving them in the selection process. Inviting the older adults to curate their own spaces is connected to contemporary work in museums and cultural institutions where groups are invited to participate in telling the stories of their own cultures and evolving selves:

> The new museology movement is largely about giving people control over their cultural heritage and its preservation as part of how they maintain, reinforce, or construct their identity. The approach acknowledges the importance of preserving not only resources that represent a community's past, but also vital elements of its living culture and its continuing development. (Kreps, 2003, p. 10)

The author goes on to define heritage as inclusive of not only the physical objects but also memories, lived experiences, and stories. All these aspects can and should be incorporated into curatorial work with older adults.

CHAPTER 9

OUR ART HISTORY

Our art history encompasses art appreciation, trips to museums and galleries, and empowerment and inclusion-oriented ways to interact with the fine art world. This chapter includes content relevant to settings with access to museums as well as those with little to no access to community art programming. It covers ways to select and consider art for discussion or stimulation—both from the canon of art history and from new and contemporary artists. As a resource for discussion, it includes some stems and prompts for facilitating art discussion groups with retired adults, those in assisted living, and elders with dementia.

Trips to Art Venues

Trips to museums and art galleries can be incredible experiences with groups of older adults. As discussed by Debono (2014), the museum can be transformed to be a "vibrant and active habitat" (p. 314) where formerly passive viewers become inhabitants of the space. Trips to museums can increase social connectedness and stimulate curiosity for older adults (Bennington et al., 2016), but not all art spaces are naturally open and welcoming for older adults. Museum settings may not be accessible due to proximity, logistics, or philosophy (Partridge, 2016a) and the art therapist should take care to design inclusive and accessible experiences when facilitating trips to art venues. Art therapists can work with care partners and community staff to extend the experience beyond the visit through discussion of related topics and other activities prior to and in the weeks after a museum trip.

Planning a Trip to an Art Venue

Though the philosophies of this book recommend approaching older adults as able and autonomous, there are some special considerations when planning a trip to an art venue to ensure a successful and valuable trip. Additionally, a scoring grid for art venues can be found in Appendix C. We use this scoring grid to assess potential venues for trips and as sites for community programs.

Prior to leaving home

Some museum security requires going through a metal detector—keep that in mind when dressing for the day.

Museums are often kept at cool temperatures to protect the art—dress in layers.

Many art spaces have hard flooring—it can be painful on older knees and feet. Suggest participants wear comfortable shoes.

Museum experiences can elicit memorable verbal responses—bring a notepad and pencil. NOTE: some museums allow pencils but no other mark-making tools.

Parking

Consider how you will get participants as close as possible to the entrance. If possible, drop the participants off at the entrance with a staff person or volunteer.

Where will you park?

How long is the trip from the car to the entrance of the art space?

Are there any accessibility issues you need to navigate?

Ticketing

Can you get tickets prior to arriving?

Are there group ticketing options or discounts for older adults?

Is there somewhere safe for the older adults to sit if you need to wait in line for tickets?

Once in the art venue

If you are attending a specific exhibit, how far is that exhibition space from the front entrance?

Where are the nearest restrooms to the exhibition space?
Are their resources for use within the exhibit or to take home for discussion afterwards?

Discussing art in the museum

In both discussion groups and trips to art venues, the framework for discussing art should be geared toward observation and creativity as opposed to the historical facts. This method is more inclusive of those with dementia or other concerns limiting or impacting verbal communication as well as more inclusive of those who have limited to no art experience. Conversations do not need to focus on pretty or well-known art; deBotton and Armstrong (2013) described the importance of discussing art we do not like, because our reactions to work we dislike can be just as important as to work we love. Though we would not do this with our clients' own work, we can model this behavior in the art museum setting—taking the first potentially transgressive step of inviting older adults to criticize or say what they do not like about a piece of art brings more freedom into the space. "I don't like this piece at all," one woman whispered to her friend, gesturing to a large minimalist painting of alternating thin stripes of color on canvas. When I invited her to speak aloud to everyone, she stood up taller, walked up to the painting and described all the things she disliked. Then she stood back for a moment and said, "But you know what? I think I don't like it because it is too exact. I have had to be so precise my whole life and I am tired of it now! Art shouldn't be so precise." Her body language and self-awareness shifted remarkably in the course of her description. Later on that same trip, she found what seemed to be the antidote to the previous piece; the canvas was similar in size and contained many of the same colors but the brush strokes were large and varied. She stood very close the canvas and made a big arc with her arm, following a splash of yellow: "This would be so fun to paint! It feels like dancing; I would love to paint like this!" As she waved her arms and gestured at the work, I noticed the previously stoic museum guard standing in the corner with a big smile on his face—her words delighted us all. Discussing work they disliked opened the door for more opinions and personal commentary. Honest discussion allows older adults, who often express guilt or discomfort about speaking up in care settings, to voice strong opinions with little chance of repercussions.

Gallery visits

Visits to art galleries or small art shows can be cost-effective and often easier to navigate than larger museums or cultural institutions. We have had success with establishing partnerships with galleries who open early for us, set up chairs, and give us special access to their exhibits. Galleries can provide the experience of being in an art venue without the higher admission cost and potentially overwhelming crowds found in larger museums. Gallery spaces might also invite consideration of more diverse materials, media, and content in art. One show we attended was an exhibit of pastoral landscapes formed from toy building blocks. Another gallery we visited on that same day involved participation in the art piece through projection and sound.

Our interactions in galleries over the years have allowed us to see and hear things I have never encountered when I visit by myself or with others my age. We have experienced incredible generosity and openness from artists and gallery owners. One art space we walked into was in the middle of an active photo shoot when we arrived. Rather than turning us away, the artists welcomed us into the space, set up chairs, and shared the food they had provided for the photography team. Several residents got to tour not only the work on display, but also the artists' workspaces. In another venue, a curator took a resident back into their storage area to see how they stored the photographic prints and negatives. He had voiced his curiosity aloud as he looked at the images on display and she immediately invited him to take a look for himself. When we work with graduating art students, we attend their senior exhibition, which allows the older adults to see a different side of the young artist they have interacted with over the year. It also allows them to give back, providing feedback and praise to the artist who has volunteered a year or more with us. Participating in larger art events is another option; many cities and communities have art walks or open studio events. Depending on the crowds, these events are wonderful ways for older adults to connect with their neighbors and to be visible in the art scene.

Public art

Public art also provides opportunities to engage with art; these types of art interactions can be structured like a driving tour to see murals (Partridge, 2016b) or unstructured through impromptu discussions of work discovered during a trip for other purposes. The relative size of public art may make it more accessible for people with vision loss. It can also be an entry point for those who may not engage in a more traditional art group. Public art with historical or cultural significance might invite those without an art background into an aesthetic discussion. As with discussing disliked art in the museum, talking about controversial public art or graffiti murals stimulates strong opinions and lively debate. The art therapist should encourage an open dialogue and encourage dissenting opinions.

The museum as continuing education

Museums and galleries can also be sites for staff engagement and continuing education. These opportunities can happen alongside the older adults; interacting in a novel environment can create situations where the caregiver to care receiver binary breaks down and people interact as coequal humans sharing an experience. Trips to see exhibits with themes or content relevant to older adults can serve as team-building as well as invite discussion of difficult topics.

The Contemporary Jewish Museum had an exhibition of the cartoonist Roz Chast (Contemporary Jewish Museum, 2017); her work covers many relatable topics, but the focus of the exhibit was her graphic memoir about her parents' aging process (Chast, 2014). I invited our company's leadership team on an afternoon trip to the museum to view and discuss the show. Nine people attended, including our vice presidents of finance, human resources, sales and marketing, and business development and strategy. I was touched by their reactions to the show even prior to any discussion—the show exhibited most of the original drawings for the book pages and I watched people moving through the exhibit alternating between laughter and tears. The trip helped to bring the mission and values of our work into focus. Chast's images enabled conversations about some of the difficult-to-navigate discussions with families. Seeing and reading about Chast's experiences in coordinating her parents' evolving medical and housing needs helped us have more understanding about the difficulty families face as they make decisions and coordinate care.

Inspired by the Death Café project started in the United Kingdom (Deathcafe.com, n.d.), I used the art museum and a shared meal as a stimulus for a discussion about death. Because of a shared responsibility to support the emotional wellness of the residents in our communities as well as to support staff experiences of grief and loss, I invited our life enrichment directors and chaplains to visit the Oakland Museum of California's exhibit for Dia de los Muertos (Oakland Museum of California, 2017). This exhibit included work relevant to grief, loss, and change. It included art installations about death, immigration, and community tragedy. We independently moved through the exhibit and then shared a meal in the museum café. As we ate, we talked about our experiences in the show, our own experiences of grief and loss, and our observations from the communities where we work. It was a time for both collaborative strategy and personal sharing.

Virtual museum visits

Advances in technology mean art venues are accessible to those who otherwise cannot make a trip to a big museum. Use of virtual reality goggles gives people the experience of not only seeing the art, but standing in the room itself (Morris, 2017; Smith, 2017). We have been experimenting with virtual reality goggles and smart phone apps providing access to museum exhibitions. The creators of one of these apps stated that the goal was to "break down the barriers that can make a gallery visit off-putting" (Smith, 2017, para. 4); the use of virtual reality to enable viewership and expose people who otherwise would not consume fine art is an exciting area for art therapists to explore. Many museums also have rich online resources and lesson plans for virtual tours. When access to these new technologies is not possible, we can use video or still-image slide shows projected onto walls or TV screens to simulate a museum visit. As technology evolves, more opportunities for these types of art encounters may be possible (Carlton, 2018).

Trips for elders with dementia

Large museums carry an element of prestige and importance; attending exhibits or tours in a large museum helps older adults with dementia to feel connected to the world around them. Increasingly, museums are developing specialized programming for people with dementia (Camic, Baker, & Tischler, 2016; Nayeri, 2018; Shaw, 2006; The I'm Still Here Foundation, n.d.), programs that question the assumptions made by caregivers about who benefits from museums (Greider, 2009). These programs typically take place when the museum is closed or in special areas of the building. Organizations working with museums and cultural institutions are also working to create programs to improve the lives of people in care partnerships with those with dementia; the House of Memories program (Ganga, Whelan, & Wilson, 2017) works on issues like empathic communication, life stories, resilience, and wellbeing.

When we took a group of residents with dementia to a large museum in San Francisco, the trip alone made a huge impact. Before we had gotten out of the van, one elder turned to me and said, "This is the most exciting day ever!" I felt it too—the infectious enthusiasm and freedom. It was a very exciting day; the elders had the entire museum to themselves and were able to voice their thoughts. I specifically asked the docents to hold back, allowing the elders to be the experts for the day. They commented about what they observed in each piece and described the work to each other. I asked open-ended questions designed to stimulate curiosity, not to quiz about facts from art history. One of the docents remarked afterwards that the older adults saw things she had never noticed in some of the work, even though she led multiple tours of the show each day. We went home, tired but satisfied. In subsequent trips to galleries and museums, I witnessed older adults and staff becoming more comfortable in the space. The need for a docent or even a structured plan began to dissipate as people relaxed and claimed the space as their own. Arriving back at the community after each of these experiences guilt set in—what about all of the elders who were not able to attend? How could we create this experience for them? I realized we needed to rethink and reimagine how we used art in our groups—especially in memory care settings. Returning to the earlier discussion of visits to galleries, if we consider the needs of the participants and want to enable greater access to art for older adults in different geographical settings, galleries may be more inclusive and enable participation with greater ease.

Art Discussion Groups

Again, as with open studio settings, this is where the art therapist's ongoing and rich art practice is essential. Beyond engaging in personal art-making, art therapists need to be connected to the larger art world. Art therapists should maintain a working awareness about current events in the fine art world, new developments or scholarship in art history, as well as connection to local art groups or organizations where applicable. This depth of understanding allows the art therapist to facilitate art discussion groups grounded in current events and to distinguish the groups from an art history lecture. Particularly with older adults, lectures can stimulate anxiety around needing to remember facts or regurgitate information. In contrast, the facilitated art discussion group can connect people to their emotions and to each other. Ideally, the art therapist is learning alongside the elders, discovering new artists and techniques and engaging in creative growth. Discussion groups with older adults have helped me to reexamine artists from the canon of art history. The elders bring their longer life experience and often bring up ideas I have never encountered in traditional art education contexts. For example, when we were discussing Pop Art and the work of Claes Oldenburg, one resident in the skilled nursing wondered aloud how viewing his giant soft sculptures of food items would feel for people who were starving or homeless. She talked about her own experiences of hunger during the Depression and the advocacy work for the homeless she did later in life. This apt criticism helped me reexamine art I had previously consumed without critique.

Before thinking about the art itself, ensure there is ample time for discussion. Older adults, like many underrepresented groups, are not often given enough time and space to process and respond: "Folks are so used to not being heard. So used to not getting their needs met" (Brown, 2017, p. 218). Brown recommended budgeting enough time for each participant to have at least five minutes. In addition to her recommendation, the facilitator needs to be able to tolerate silences—to wait long enough for the participants to think and then respond. Group settings can be particularly challenging to older adults with hearing loss; they have to exert more effort to process what they hear and differentiate communicative sound from background noise (Gosselin & Gagné, 2011). This wait time may extend even longer when older adults are processing a new idea or encountering new work.

When choosing art to discuss, consider the formal elements of the art as well as the potential emotional and intellectual content. I have had success with both representational and non-representational work, both ancient and contemporary. Prompted by direct requests from older adults (Partridge, 2016a), I often incorporate art with provocative content or art forms outside the traditional canon of accepted media and materials. Even in otherwise conservative settings, we have rich, nuanced discussions of contemporary art. The only rules I suggest are related to vision and the qualities of the space. Consider any sensory impairment among the group participants; certain vision decline may limit the accessibility of images with low contrast or small details. Depending on the setting and group size, I may incorporate visual projection or printed copies of the images to be discussed. Particularly for older adults with dementia, having a physical copy to hold will assist the older adults in participating in the discussion.

Occasionally, I will choose just two images from one artist and focus our discussion on the two images. In a discussion of the artist Jack Witten's work in the week after his death (Genzlinger, 2018; Greenberger, 2018), some residents had very strong feelings about which of the two they preferred, and what the pieces meant. I generally provide a small amount of biographical information, but in the case of this artist, and because I knew about some pressing concerns for the residents present at the group, I provided more of a rich context. The two pieces I brought for our group, "Dead Reckoning I" (1980) and "Apps for Obama" (2011), were very different in color and composition. We discussed his participation in the civil rights movement and the fact that he was unrecognized for much of his career. One woman related to both pieces as parts of herself. She held the printed copies of the paintings on either side of her head and said, "I am right here in the middle of these two." She stated that the painting "Apps for Obama" (2011) depicted the human experience of possessing "little bits of knowledge about a lot of things, but none of it is complete." This resident often described herself that way—a registered nurse, a teacher, and a leader, but never an expert. She had a difficult family history and was struggling to connect to her peers in the assisted living because she felt pulled between caring for them and

113

accepting care herself. A recent change requiring total reliance on her wheelchair amplified her struggle for autonomy and empowerment; she described feeling pulled between the darkness inside her and the desire to focus on positive aspects of life.

As we continued to discuss the two paintings and the artist, the group members voiced increasingly nuanced opinions, some expressed through gesture and hand motions. With their fingers, they jabbed at the parts they liked best and blocked off the areas they did not like. They moved their fingers back and forth between the different elements in the paintings, making connections and identifying symmetries. Most importantly, not a single person asked what the paintings meant or looked for a definitive answer; they were confident in their own thoughts and definitions.

Responding to art

Occasionally, we used the art discussion groups as inspiration points for our own creative practice. The neighborhood scenes from the artist Jacob Lawrence have served as incredible starting points for discussions about what creates a sense of home, reminiscing about past homes, and discussions of congregate living—something many of them are experiencing for the first time since college or military service. I have used his work many times as an inspiration point in art therapy groups for older adults in assisted living. One woman stayed to participate in a discussion of Lawrence's art because of her interest in the poetry of the Harlem Renaissance. She had been a magazine and newspaper editor with a deep love for the written word. Though she usually wheeled herself away once we started our art responses, she stayed to participate after seeing and discussing this work. For this art response directive, I invite participants to create their own building or house shapes or to work with simple shapes I provide for them. Depending on the group members, I either provide pre-cut people or I set out magazines for collage. Especially for the themes of this project, I supply a diverse collection of human images, making sure the images represent a wide range of ages, ethnicities, abilities, facial expressions, gestures, and body postures. I invite participants to populate their images with community, however they imagine it. This elder, who traditionally did not create images, added a few people into the windows of the building. Then she wrote big numbers on the front of the building, above the door.

She gasped aloud after she finished writing, and told us she had not remembered until just that moment the address number for the building where she lived in Washington, DC. The art process had stimulated the memory. She went on to describe all her neighbors in the building and the connection she felt to the building and the community the building contained. Her piece led us into a discussion about the building they all currently occupied as a container for community.

Suggested questions for art discussion groups

- Where do you look first?

- What are you curious about?

- Which of these pieces seem to be in a conversation with each other?

- What similarities or differences can you find in these pieces of art?

- If we could take one of these pieces home with us, which would you choose? Where would we display it?

- Which one do you wish you created?

- Which one is your least favorite? Why? What would you change about it?

- If the people in these two paintings could talk to each other, what would they say?

The idea behind making art history or art appreciation "our art history" enables the older adults to rewrite and reframe creative expressions. We break down the barriers between those who like art and those who do not. Facilitating these groups in such a way that they invite people to voice unpopular or critical ideas engages older adults in a productive process of cultural critique. It invites them to take an active role in redefining what art means and how to understand it. The idea of "our art history" supports the philosophy of approaching older adults as artists and creative people.

CHAPTER 10

CONCLUSION

Art therapy with older adults is about so much more than the small spaces it has been confined to in the past. Shifting toward empowerment and connection invites art therapists to collaborate with older adults instead of treating them as patients or doing things for them. Art therapists need to do the sometimes complicated but incredibly rewarding work to create space, show up, and invite the older adults in as artists. Empowerment has been implicated in better outcomes in rehabilitation work with older adults (Gol karami, Mobaraki, Kamali, & Farhodi, 2013). As we work to better understand the impacts of loneliness, social isolation, and purpose in life, we need more ways to support the holistic wellness of older adults as they age. Part of gaining this new knowledge means asking the older adults themselves: What do they need? What do they hope for? How can we get out of their way in the pursuit of contentment and creativity?

The approach described in this book is essential in the work to counter alarmist, discriminatory messages about the older adult population (Applewhite, 2016; Cruikshank, 2013; Sweetland & Volmert, 2017); older adults are not a "danger to the common good" (Cruikshank, 2013, p. 26). Though the negative messages address population shifts and care needs, which are realities, approaching older adults from a perspective of growth as opposed to illness and treatment can assist with changing the discussion. The FrameWorks Institute suggests eliminating the "us versus them" approaches, instead focusing on what we do together (Sweetland & Volmert, 2017); this research-backed approach connects directly to the philosophy of art therapy with older adults presented in this book.

Breaking Away from Bingo

I feel very concerned when I hear students and new professionals speak about reluctance or refusal to work with older adults. I have come to understand it as an unfortunate combination of assumptions on the part of the art therapist and a failure of the imagination of the elder care industry. The efforts to change cultures and practices in older adult care settings are not easy nor a straight line. It may mean challenging long-established practices. The most pernicious, in my experience, is bingo. In proposing a drastic overhaul of our community program, I had to do some self-inquiry as well, to understand what people hear when I criticize bingo. I created mixed-media paintings on old bingo cards as part of this self-inquiry. The reaction from others may have been fear of my judgment and part internalized ageism. It could also be lack of awareness about other possibilities. My bingo card art project helped me to understand the situation from multiple vantage points and to adjust my approach when proposing changes.

Though we love and are passionate about the work we do, we need to be careful when bringing art therapy and this empowerment approach into new settings. The art therapist needs to be aware of the potential discomfort art therapy introduces into the community. What long-held beliefs are challenged? What discomfort does invoking therapy stimulate? What biases exist within the organization that stand in the way of new ideas or only fund and sustain programming with instant results? I have seen transformative shifts in individuals and organizations, but the shifts do not happen instantly.

Art therapists often need to advocate for themselves and for their profession when employed in these settings (Partridge, 2016c, 2017, 2018), particularly if they are the first or only art therapist working there. This advocacy can include boundary setting about group size, how others in the setting understand and describe the work of the art therapist, and what materials and space are needed for effective and ethical practice. Art therapists who accept non-traditional roles may be able to engage in job crafting (Wrzesniewski, Berg, & Dutton, 2010; Wrzesniewski & Dutton, 2001) as a means to shape their workplace role in the best interests of the communities and populations the art therapist works with. The older adults are also excellent advocates for art therapy.

Synthesis of the Approaches

A series of experiences in one community synthesizes many of the approaches and philosophies presented in this book. During an art discussion group in a skilled nursing setting, we discussed the work of Jane Kim, a science illustrator and muralist. We viewed the video of her work on the Wall of Birds (Monoyios, 2016; Zoellner, 2015) and looked at some of her other images. Her work, like Chapter 6, Projects with Purpose, is intended to deliver a message or stimulate dialogue habitat and species conservation. Doing so in mural form, as discussed in Chapter 7, allowed Kim to speak to larger audiences. The participants, including both residents and family members, were in awe of both the artistic skill and the social impact of her work.

Several months later, I attended an event at the deYoung Museum. Kim was the artist in residence that month and happened to be in the residency gallery. After participating in her project, I went up and introduced myself. I told her how impactful her work had been to the older adults and how much they enjoyed seeing her projects. Her immediate response was to ask if she could come meet them. She also expressed interest in seeing the work we created together.

The day she was scheduled to visit, the residents and I set up an exhibition of their work. Using tables draped in white tablecloths, we arranged their completed and in-progress pieces. Each artist selected and set out their own work, making choices about what they hoped to show to our visiting artist. Residents from memory care, assisted living, and skilled nursing along with family and staff filled the room. Many of the participants from the initial discussion group were in the front row. Kim gave a beautiful overview of her work. She shared the process behind each project as well as her path to becoming a muralist and science illustrator. After answering their questions, she asked them to show her their art. She spent time with each resident, hearing about their work, their interests, and their roles in our creative community. Reflecting on the experience, I created a response piece with a sketch of one of the older adult artists, arm in arm with our visitor (Figure 10.1).

Figure 10.1 One of the most touching moments from the lecture and art show was one of the older adult artists who linked arms with Kim and gave her a tour of the show. She described not only her own work, but also the work of her peers.

The feather in my response image represents both the initial connection to Kim's work through the Wall of Birds and the delicate beauty of the experience we all shared. I chose not to glue the glitter, feather, or drawing to the surface as a symbolic hope that this experience can be repeated in many settings with different groups of intergenerational artists; the elements in this image can be changed, moved around, and new groups of people can enter the composition. The two artists have their heads close together as they talk and view art—gray hair merging into black hair. There were no barriers between "professional" artists and "resident" artists that afternoon—we were all creative people sharing our lives and our art. Opportunities like this one work to break down the artificial separation of groups of people by age and generational labels.

Reciprocal Empowerment

In discussing the book title and intention with some older adults, one resident said, "Well you empower us—you empower us with art, that's exactly what you do." They often express their gratitude for the ways that art therapy and our interactions have impacted their lives—what they may never fully understand is the way the interactions with them have changed my life. When I began this work, I had no idea how many incredible opportunities it would open up, how many phenomenal people I would meet, or the way it would influence my work as an artist and art therapist. Each older adult I have interacted with left a mark on me; they are so generous in sharing their life experiences. The work presented here would not have been possible without the collaborative assistance from care partners, family members, and other professionals in the field of aging; they too have been my teachers. Though my goal is to support spaces where the older adults can connect and feel empowered, I have found it does just as much to connect and empower everyone who interacts in our creative space, including myself. To transform the world to be more inclusive of all of us, we need to facilitate spaces where we all create and interact together.

Appendices

Appendix A: Participation Rubric

Older Adult Participation Rubric

Passive Participation (PP)	Older adult is present in room for at least 10 minutes, but does not verbalize, make eye contact, or otherwise respond to peers, art therapist, or others in the room.
Moderate Participation (MP)	Older adult is present in the room for at least 10 minutes. Older adult interacts with peers, art therapist, or others in the room via verbalization, eye contact or gesture.
Active Participation (AP)	Older adult is present in the room for greater than 20 minutes. Older adult interacts with peers, art therapist, or others in the room via verbalization, eye contact or gesture. Older adult participates in verbal conversation or art process via verbalization, eye contact, or gesture.
Decline to Participate (DP)	Older adult is invited to attend, but declines. **OR** Older adult attends, but is present for less than 10 minutes.

Appendix B: An Older Adult Is Scale

Please create a representation of an older adult using line/shape/color.

TITLE: _____

Complete the following statements:

An older adult is _____ .

An older adult can _____ .

An older adult and I _____ .

Appendix C: Art Space Scoring Grid

Art space scoring for _____

Accessibility	Excellent (3)	Adequate (2)	Difficult (1)
Transportation			
Parking			
Distance to entrance			
Distance from entrance to exhibition			
Restroom access			
Seating availability			
Lighting/other vision concerns			
Other physical access concerns			
Accessibility notes:			
Total accessibility score:			

Information/resources	Excellent (3)	Adequate (2)	Difficult (1)
Availability of docents			
Docents with specific training for work with older adults			
Docents with specific training for work with people with dementia			
Information about exhibition			
Information about artists/artwork			

Interactive elements			
Resources for use after visit/continued learning			

Information/resources category notes:

Total information/resources score: |

Other considerations	Excellent (3)	Adequate (2)	Difficult (1)
Cost			
Calendar/program variety			
Calendar/program updates			

Other category notes:

Total other considerations score: |

Total score:	

Notes: _____

Address: _____

Phone number: _____

Contact person: _____ Email: _____

REFERENCES

Abraham, R. (2005). When words have lost their meaning: Alzheimer's patients communicate through art. Westport, CT: Praeger.

Abramowitz, K. (2013). The unstructured use of clay in art therapy with older adults. Canadian Art Therapy Association Journal, 26(1), 1–13.

Adamowicz, E. (1998). Surrealist collage in text and image: Dissecting the exquisite corpse. Cambridge, UK: Cambridge University Press.

Allen, P. B. (1995). Art is a way of knowing. Boston, MA: Shambhala.

American Psychological Association. (2010). Publication manual of the American Psychological Association. Washington, DC: American Psychological Association.

American Psychological Association. (2014). Guidelines for psychological practice with older adults. American Psychologist, 69(1), 34–65. http://doi.org/10.1037/a0035063

Anderson, T., & Conlon, B. (2013). In the shadow of the Peace Walls: Art, education, and social reconstruction in Northern Ireland. Art Education, 66(4), 36–43.

Applewhite, A. (2016). This chair rocks: A manifesto against ageism. Farmington Hills, MI: Thorndike Press.

Argue, J., Bennett, J., & Gussak, D. (2009). Transformation through negotiation: Initiating the Inmate Mural Arts Program. The Arts in Psychotherapy, 36(5), 313–319. http://doi.org/10.1016/j.aip.2009.07.005

Atkins, S., & Williams, L. D. (2007). Sourcebook in expressive arts therapy. Boone, NC: Parkway Publishers Inc. http://doi.org/10.1017/CBO9781107415324.004

Baca, J. (2009). Judy Baca: Public memory. Public Art Review, 20(2), 28–30.

Backos, A. (2018). Philosophical foundations of art therapy. In R. Carolan & A. Backos (Eds.), Emerging perspectives in art therapy: Trends, movements, and developments (pp. 3–16). New York, NY: Routledge.

Beauchet, O., Launay, C. P., Merjagnan, C., Kabeshova, A., & Annweiler, C. (2014). Quantified self and comprehensive geriatric assessment: Older adults are able to evaluate their own health and functional status. PloS One, 9(6), 1–10. http://doi.org/10.1371/journal.pone.0100636

Bennington, R., Backos, A., Harrison, J., Etherington Reader, A., & Carolan, R. (2016). Art therapy in art museums: Promoting social connectedness and psychological well-being of older adults. The Arts in Psychotherapy, 49, 34–43. http://doi.org/10.1016/j.aip.2016.05.013

Berberian, M. (2003). Communal rebuilding after destruction: The World Trade Center children's mural project. Psychoanalytic Social Work, 10(1), 27–41. http://doi.org/10.1300/J032v10n01_04

Berger, S. (2012). Is my world getting smaller? The challenges of living with vision loss. Journal of Vision Impairment and Blindness, 106(1), 5–17.

Berry, P., Mascia, J., & Steinman, B. A. (2004). Vision and hearing loss in older adults: "Double trouble." Care Management Journals, 5(1), 35–40.

Bober, S. J., McLellan, E., McBee, L., & Westreich, L. (2002). The Feelings Art Group: A vehicle for personal expression in skilled nursing home residents with dementia. Journal of Social Work in Long-Term Care, 1(4), 73–87.

Bonanno, G. A., Neria, Y., Mancini, A., Coifman, K. G., Litz, B., & Insel, B. (2007). Is there more to complicated grief than depression and posttraumatic stress disorder? A test of incremental validity. Journal of Abnormal Psychology, 116(2), 342–351. http://doi.org/10.1037/0021-843X.116.2.342

Boudreaux, E. O., Cherry, K. E., Elliott, E. M., & Hicks, J. L. (2011). Effects of distraction and pictorial illustration on memory for countries in older adults with probable Alzheimer's disease. Experimental Aging Research, 37(3), 293–309. http://doi.org/10.1080/03610 73X.2011.568816

Bradford Dementia Group. (2008). The Bradford well-being profile. Retrieved September 20, 2018 from https://www.bradford.ac.uk/health/media/facultyofhealthstudies/Bradford-Well-Being-Profile-with-cover-(3).pdf

Brown, A. M. (2017). Emergent strategy. Chico, CA: AK Press.

Brown, C. (2008). Very toxic—Handle with care. Some aspects of the maternal function in art therapy. International Journal of Art Therapy, 13(1), 13–24. http://doi.org/10.1080/17454830802069935

Buettner, L. (1995). Therapeutic recreation in the nursing home. State College, PA: Venture Pub.

Burling, S. (2018, April 3). Old and ageist: Why so many older people have prejudices about their peers—and themselves. The Inquirer, pp. 1–6. Retrieved September 20, 2018 from www.philly.com/philly/health/old-and-ageist-why-do-so-many-older-people-have-prejudices-about-their-peers-and-themselves-20180404.html

Byers, A. (2011). Visual aesthetics in dementia. International Journal of Art Therapy, 16(2), 81–89. http://doi.org/10.1080/17454832.2011.602980

Camic, P. M., Baker, E. L., & Tischler, V. (2016). Theorizing how art gallery interventions impact people with dementia and their caregivers. Gerontologist, 56(6), 1033–1041. http://doi.org/10.1093/geront/gnv063

Carlton, N. (2018). Transcending media: Tangible to digital and their mixed reality. In R. Carolan & A. Backos (Eds.), Emerging perspectives in art therapy: Trends, movements, and developments (pp. 74–90). New York, NY: Routledge.

Carolan, R. (2001). Models and paradigms of art therapy research. Art Therapy, 18(4), 190–206. http://doi.org/10.1080/07421656.2001.10129537

Carolan, R., & Backos, A. (Eds.). (2018). Emerging perspectives in art therapy. New York, NY: Routledge.

Carstensen, L. L., Pasupathi, M., Mayr, U., & Nesselroade, J. R. (2000). Emotional experience in everyday life across the adult life span. Journal of Personality and Social Psychology, 79(4), 644–655.

Chast, R. (2014). Can't we talk about something more pleasant? New York, NY: Bloomsbury.

Chilton, G. (2007). Altered books in art therapy with adolescents. Art Therapy, 24(2), 59–63. http://doi.org/10.1080/07421656.2007.10129588

Chilton, G., Gerity, L., LaVorgna-Smith, M., & MacMichael, H. N. (2009). An online art exchange group: 14 secrets for a happy artist's life. Art Therapy, 26(2), 66–72. http://doi.org/10.1080/07421656.2009.10129741

Clover, D. (2011). Successes and challenges of feminist arts-based participatory methodologies with homeless/street-involved women in Victoria. Action Research, 9(1), 12–26. http://doi.org/10.1177/1476750310396950

Coffey, M. K. (2012). How a revolutionary art became official culture: Murals, museums, and the Mexican state. Durham, NC: Duke University Press.

Cohen-Mansfield, J., Thein, K., Dakheel-Ali, M., & Marx, M. S. (2010). Engaging nursing home residents with dementia in activities: The effects of modeling, presentation order, time of day, and setting characteristics. Aging & Mental Health, 14(4), 471–480. http://doi.org/10.1080/13607860903586102

Contemporary Jewish Museum (2017). Roz Chast: Cartoon memoirs. Retrieved March 19, 2018, from https://thecjm.org/exhibitions/66

Creative Aging International (2016). About us. Retrieved February 19, 2018, from www.creativeageinginternational.com/about-us

Cruikshank, M. (2013). Learning to be old: Gender, culture, and aging (3rd ed.). Lanham, MD: Rowman & Littlefield Publishers, Inc.

Czamanski-Cohen, J. (2010). "Oh! Now I remember": The use of a studio approach to art therapy with internally displaced people. Arts in Psychotherapy, 37(5), 407–413. http://doi.org/10.1016/j.aip.2010.09.003

Davis, K. M., & Atkins, S. S. (2009). Ecotherapy: Tribalism in the mountains and forest. Journal of Creativity in Mental Health, 4(3), 273–282. http://doi.org/10.1080/15401380903192747

Deathcafe.com (n.d.). What is Death Cafe? Retrieved April 9, 2018, from http://deathcafe.com/what

Debono, S. (2014). Rethinking national art museums and the values of community curation. Malta Review of Educational Research, 8(2), 312–320.

deBotton, A., & Armstrong, J. (2013). Art as therapy. London, UK: Phaidon Press.

Deloof, J. (n.d.). Arts Network Manual. Retrieved September 20, 2018 from https://namica.org/get-involved/anti-stigma-arts-network/anti-stigma-arts-manual

Desmyter, F., & De Raedt, R. (2012). The relationship between time perspective and subjective well-being of older adults. Psychologica Belgica, 52(1), 19–38. http://doi.org/10.5334/pb-52-1-19

Diachun, L. L., Charise, A., & Lingard, L. (2012). Old news: Why the 90-year crisis in medical elder care? Journal of the American Geriatrics Society, 60(7), 1357–1360. http://doi.org/10.1111/j.1532-5415.2012.04029.x

Dissanayake, E. (1995a). 1994 keynote address reflecting on the past: Implications of prehistory and infancy for art therapy. Art Therapy, 12(1), 17–23. http://doi.org/10.1080/07421656.1995.10759119

Dissanayake, E. (1995b). Homo aestheticus: Where art comes from and why. Seattle, WA: University of Washington Press.

Eden Alternative. (2013). It can be different. Retrieved September 20, 2018 from www.edenalt.org/wordpress/wp-content/uploads/2014/02/Eden_Overview_092613LR.pdf

Edmunds, J. D. (2012). The applications and implications of digital media in art therapy: A survey study. Philadelphia, PA: Drexel University.

Eekelaar, C., Camic, P. M., & Springham, N. (2012). Art galleries, episodic memory and verbal fluency in dementia: An exploratory study. Psychology of Aesthetics, Creativity, and the Arts, 6(3), 262–272. http://doi.org/10.1037/a0027499

Ehresman, C. (2014). From rendering to remembering: Art therapy for people with Alzheimer's disease. International Journal of Art Therapy, 19(1), 43–51. http://doi.org/10.1080/17454832.2013.819023

Eldon, D., & Eldon, K. (1997). The journey is the destination: The journals of Dan Eldon. San Francisco, CA: Chronicle Books.

Eligon, J., & Cooper, M. (2013, April 15). Blasts at Boston Marathon kill 3 and injure 100. The New York Times. Retrieved September 20, 2018 from www.nytimes.com/2013/04/16/us/explosions-reported-at-site-of-boston-marathon.html

Erikson, J. M. (1988). Wisdom and the senses: The way of creativity. New York, NY: W. W. Norton.

Fawcett, J., Clark, D. C., Scheftner, W. A., & Gibbons, R. D. (1983). Assessing anhedonia in psychiatric patients: The pleasure scale. Archives of General Psychiatry, 40(1), 79–84.

Fish, B. J. (2012). Response art: The art of the art therapist. Art Therapy: Journal of the American Art Therapy Association, 29(3), 138–143. http://doi.org/10.1080/074216 56.2012.701594

Foster, T., Galjour, C., & Spengel, S. (2015). Investigating holistic wellness dimensions during older adulthood: A factor analytic study. Journal of Adult Development, 22(4), 239–247. http://doi.org/10.1007/s10804-015-9215-4

Fry, P. S., & Debats, D. L. (2014). Sources of life strengths appraisal scale: A multidimensional approach to assessing older adults' perceived sources of life strengths. Journal of Aging Research, 1–15. http://doi.org/10.1155/2014/783637

Funk & Wagnalls New World Encyclopedia (2014). Parkinson's disease. In Funk & Wagnalls New World Encyclopedia (p. 1). Chicago, IL: World Book, Inc.

Galbraith, A., Subrin, R., & Ross, D. (2008). Alzheimer's disease: Art, creativity and the brain. In N. Hass-Cohen & S. M. D. Carr (Eds.), Art therapy and clinical neuroscience (pp. 254–267). London, UK: Jessica Kingsley Publishers.

Galoustian, G. (2018, February 21). Intervention helps couples affected by Alzheimer's Disease. Florida Atlantic University News Desk. Retrieved February 22, 2018, from www.fau.edu/ newsdesk/articles/ad-couples-study.php

Ganga, R. N., Whelan, G., & Wilson, K. (2017). Evaluation of the House of Memories family carers awareness day. Liverpool, UK: Institute of Cultural Capital.

Geller, S. (2013). Sparking the creative in older adults. Psychological Perspectives: A Quarterly Journal of Jungian Aging and Individuation, 56, 200–211. http://doi.org/10.1080/00 332925.2013.786974

Genzlinger, N. (2018, January 23). Jack Whitten, artist of wide-ranging curiosity, dies at 78. New York Times. Retrieved September 20, 2018 from https://nyti.ms/2F7BS7A

Ghesquiere, A. (2014). "I was just trying to stick it out until I realized that I couldn't": A phenomenological investigation of support seeking among older adults with complicated grief. OMEGA—Journal of Death and Dying, 68(1), 1–22. http://doi.org/10.2190/ OM.68.1.a

Goalwin, G. (2013). The art of war: Instability, insecurity, and ideological imagery in Northern Ireland's political murals, 1979–1998. International Journal of Politics, Culture and Society, 26(3), 189–215. http://doi.org/10.1007/s10767-013-9142-y

Gol karami, S. H., Mobaraki, H., Kamali, M., & Farhodi, F. (2013). The effect of empowerment programs on geriatric depression in daily rehabilitation Farzanegan center of Khorramabad city. Modern Rehabilitation, 6(4), 65–70.

Gosselin, P. A., & Gagné, J. P. (2011). Older adults expend more listening effort than young adults recognizing speech in noise. Journal of Speech, Language, and Hearing Research, 54(3), 944–958. http://doi.org/10.1044/1092-4388(2010/10-0069)a

Greenberger, A. (2018, January). Jack Whitten, beloved painter of abstract cosmologies, dies at 78. ARTnews. Retrieved September 20, 2018 from www.artnews.com/2018/01/21/ jack-whitten-beloved-painter-abstract-cosmologies-dies-78

Greider, L. (2009, October). In museums, those with Alzheimer's find themselves again. AARP Bulletin Today. Retrieved September 20, 2018 from www.aarp.org/health/brain-health/ info-10-2009/in_museums_those_with_alzheimer_s_find_themselves_again.html

Guggenheim (2018). Rirkrit Tiravanija. Retrieved February 19, 2018, from www.guggenheim. org/artwork/artist/rirkrit-tiravanija

Halpern, A. R., & O'Connor, M. G. (2013). Stability of art preference in frontotemporal dementia. Psychology of Aesthetics, Creativity, and the Arts, 7(1), 95–99. http://doi. org/10.1037/a0031734

Harrison, S. W. (2000). Spilling open: The art of becoming yourself. New York, NY: Villard Books.

Heine, C., & Browning, C. J. (2004). The communication and psychosocial perceptions of older adults with sensory loss: A qualitative study. Ageing and Society, 24(1), 113–130. http://doi.org/10.1017/S0144686X03001491

Hensley, P. L. (2006). A review of bereavement-related depression and complicated grief. Psychiatric Annals, 39(9), 618–627.

Hinz, L. D. (2017). The ethics of art therapy: Promoting creativity as a force for positive change. Art Therapy, 34(3), 142–145. http://doi.org/10.1080/07421656.2017.1343073

Holstein, M. B., & Minkler, M. (2003). Self, society, and the "new gerontology." The Gerontologist, 43(6), 787–796.

Houpt, K., Balkin, L. "Ariella," Broom, R. H., Roth, A. G., & Selma. (2016). Anti-memoir: Creating alternate nursing home narratives through zine making. Art Therapy, 33(3), 128–137. http://doi.org/10.1080/07421656.2016.1199243

Hubalek, S. K. (1997). I can't draw a straight line: Bringing art into the lives of older adults. Baltimore, MD: Health Professions Press, Inc.

Huebner, B. G. (2012). I remember better when I paint. Glen Echo, MD: Bethesda Communications Group.

Huet, V. (2015). Literature review of art therapy-based interventions for work-related stress. International Journal of Art Therapy: Inscape, 20(2), 66–76. http://doi.org/10.1080/17454832.2015.1023323

Huet, V. (2017). Case study of an art therapy-based group for work-related stress with hospice staff. International Journal of Art Therapy: Inscape, 22(1), 22–34. http://doi.org/10.1080/17454832.2016.1260039

Jernigan, C. (1999). Evidence: The art of Candy Jernigan. San Francisco, CA: Chronicle Books.

Jue, J. (2017). The extent of engagement in art making and exhibition by art therapy practitioners and students. Arts in Psychotherapy, 55, 32–39. http://doi.org/10.1016/j.aip.2017.04.004

Kaimal, G., & Gerber, N. (2007). Impressions over time: Community progressive murals in an outpatient HIV/AIDS clinic. Arts in Psychotherapy, 34(2), 151–162. http://doi.org/10.1016/j.aip.2007.01.002

Kaimal, G., Mensinger, J. L., Drass, J. M., & Dieterich-Hartwell, R. M. (2017). Art therapist-facilitated open studio versus coloring: Differences in outcomes of affect, stress, creative agency, and self-efficacy. Canadian Art Therapy Association Journal, 30(2), 56–68. http://doi.org/10.1080/08322473.2017.1375827

Kaiser, D., & Deaver, S. (2013). Establishing a research agenda for art therapy: A Delphi study. Art Therapy: Journal of the American Art Therapy Association, 30(3), 114–121. http://doi.org/10.1080/07421656.2013.819281

Keedwell, P. A., Andrew, C., Williams, S. C. R., Brammer, M. J., & Phillips, M. L. (2005). The neural correlates of anhedonia in major depressive disorder. Biological Psychiatry, 58(11), 843–853. http://doi.org/10.1016/j.biopsych.2005.05.019

Kerchner, G. A., Racine, C. A., Hale, S., Wilheim, R., Laluz, V., Miller, B. L., & Kramer, J. H. (2012). Cognitive processing speed in older adults: Relationship with white matter integrity. PLoS One, 7(11). http://doi.org/10.1371/journal.pone.0050425

Khil, L., Wellmann, J., & Berger, K. (2015). Impact of combined sensory impairments on health-related quality of life. Quality of Life Research: An International Journal of Quality of Life Aspects of Treatment, Care and Rehabilitation, 24, 2099–2103. http://doi.org/10.1007/s11136-015-0941-7

Kincaid, C., & Peacock, J. R. (2003). The effect of a wall mural on decreasing four types of door-testing behaviors. Journal of Applied Gerontology, 22(1), 76–88. http://doi.org/10.1177/0733464802250046

Kopytin, A. I., & Rugh, M. M. (Eds.). (2016). Green studio: Nature and the arts in therapy. Hauppage, NY: Nova Science Publishers, Inc.

Kreps, C. F. (2003). Liberating culture: Cross-cultural perspectives on museums, curation and heritage preservation. New York, NY: Routledge.

Ladd, K. L., Merluzzi, T. V., & Cooper, D. (2006). Retirement issues for Roman Catholic priests: A theoretical and qualitiative investigation. Review of Religious Research, 48(1), 82–105.

Lamb, S. (2014). Permanent personhood or meaningful decline? Toward a critical anthropology of successful aging. Journal of Aging Studies, 29(1), 41–52. http://doi.org/10.1016/j. jaging.2013.12.006

Lancioni, G. E., Perilli, V., Singh, N. N., O'Reilly, M. F., & Cassano, G. (2011). A man with severe Alzheimer's disease stops wandering during a picture colouring activity. Developmental Neurorehabilitation, 14(August), 242–246. http://doi.org/10.3109/17518423.2011.5 75439

Landgarten, H. (1987). Family art psychotherapy: A clinical guide and casebook. New York, NY: Brunner/Mazel.

Latorre, G. (2008). Murals and postmodernism: Post-movimiento, heterogeneity, and new media in Chicana/o indigenism. In Walls of empowerment: Chicana/o indigenist murals of California (pp. 211–239). Austin, TX: University of Texas Press.

Leverenz, J., Grimes, R., & Partridge, E. (2013). Plenary session. In Art therapy: Connecting visual expression and healing. Seattle, WA.

Lewis, G. (1979). Adler's theory of personality and art therapy in a nursing home. Art Psychotherapy, 6, 47–50.

Liebmann, M. (1986). Art therapy for groups: A handbook of themes, games, and exercises. Cambridge, MA: Brookline Books.

Low, W. H. (1902). Mural painting: Modern possibilities of an ancient art. Brush and Pencil, 11(3), 161–177.

Lu, L., & Yuen, F. (2012). Journey women: Art therapy in a decolonizing framework of practice. The Arts in Psychotherapy, 39(3), 192–200. http://doi.org/10.1016/j.aip.2011.12.007

Lundebjerg, N. E., Trucil, D. E., Hammond, E. C., & Applegate, W. B. (2017). When it comes to older adults, language matters: Journal of the American Geriatrics Society adopts modified American Medical Association style. Journal of the American Geriatrics Society, 65(7), 1386–1388. http://doi.org/10.1111/jgs.14941

Marshall, S. (2017). On measuring the subtleties of change: A reflection on small-scale evaluation in arts therapies work with adults with learning disabilities. International Journal of Art Therapy: Inscape, 22(2), 57–63. http://doi.org/10.1080/17454832.20 17.1296477

Mather, M. (2006). A review of decision-making processes: Weighing the risks and benefits of aging. In L. L. Carstensen & C. R. Hartel (Eds.), When I'm 64. (pp. 145–173). Washington, DC: The National Academies Press. http://doi.org/10.1017/CBO9781107415324.004

McKenna, K., & Grattan, N. (2012). Jesse Houlding. Retrieved March 19, 2018, from http:// inthemake.com/jesse-houlding

Menon, E. K. (2004). Anatomy of a motif: The fetus in late 19th-century graphic art. Nineteenth-Century Art Worldwide, 3(1), 1–24.

Metropolitan Museum of Art. (n.d.). Claude Monet, Haystacks (Effect of Snow and Sun). Retrieved September 20, 2018 from www.metmuseum.org/art/collection/search/437122

Miller, L. (n.d.). A bus to nowhere. Radiolab. Retrieved September 20, 2018 from www. radiolab.org/story/121385-bus-nowhere

Monoyios, K. (2016, January). 516 bird feet in 3,000 square feet. Scientific American Blog. Retrieved September 20, 2018 from https://blogs.scientificamerican.com/ symbiartic/516-bird-feet-in-3-000-square-feet

Moon, B. L. (2016). The sirens of definition: Responding to the call. Art Therapy, 33(3), 156–159. http://doi.org/10.1080/07421656.2016.1199247

Moon, C. (2002). Studio art therapy: Cultivating the artist identity in the art therapist. Philadelphia, PA: Jessica Kingsley Publishers.

Morris, I. (2017, September). Experience art in VR, from your iPhone, with ArtPassport. Forbes. Retrieved September 20, 2018 from www.forbes.com/sites/ianmorris/2017/09/14/experience-art-in-vr-from-your-iphone-with-artpassport/#38a39e5c372e

National Endowment for the Arts; National Center For Creative Aging. (2016). The summit on creativity and aging in America. Washington, DC: The National Endowment for the Arts Office of Accessibility.

Nayeri, F. (2018, March 11). Museums fight the isolation and pain of dementia. The New York Times, pp. 11–13.

Nelson, T. D. (2005). Ageism: Prejudice against our feared future self. Journal of Social Issues, 61(2), 207–221. http://doi.org/10.1111/j.1540-4560.2005.00402.x

Oakland Museum of California (2017). Metamorphosis and migration: Days of the dead. Retrieved March 19, 2018, from http://museumca.org/exhibit/days-of-the-dead-2017

O'Neil, M., & Haydon, A. (2015). Aging, agency, and attribution of responsibility: Shifting public discourse about older adults. Retrieved September 20, 2018 from www.frameworksinstitute.org/assets/files/aging_ffa_final_090215.pdf

Ong, A. D., Benson, L., Zautra, A. J., & Ram, N. (2017). Emotion emodiversity and biomarkers of inflammation. Emotion, 18(1), 3–14. http://doi.org/10.1037/emo0000343

Orgeta, V., Edwards, R. T., Hounsome, B., Orrell, M., & Woods, B. (2015). The use of the EQ-5D as a measure of health-related quality of life in people with dementia and their carers. Quality of Life Research: An International Journal of Quality of Life Aspects of Treatment, Care and Rehabilitation, 24(2), 315–324. http://doi.org/10.1007/s11136-014-0770-0

Ottemiller, D. D., & Awais, Y. J. (2016). A model for art therapists in community-based practice. Art Therapy, 33(3), 144–150. http://doi.org/10.1080/07421656.2016.1199245

Paivio, A. (2014). Intelligence, dual coding theory, and the brain. Intelligence, 47, 141–158. http://doi.org/10.1016/j.intell.2014.09.002

Paivio, A., & Sadoski, M. (2011). Lexicons, contexts, events, and images: Commentary on Elman (2009) from the perspective of dual coding theory. Cognitive Science, 35(1), 198–209. http://doi.org/10.1111/j.1551-6709.2010.01146.x

Partridge, E. E. (2010, November). Personal hope book: Bringing light into the forensic setting. Poster presented at Awakening Awareness: American Art Therapy Association Annual Conference. Sacramento, CA.

Partridge, E. E. (2011, November). Personal hope book: A container of resilience. Workshop presented at the Expressive Therapies Summit. New York, NY.

Partridge, E. E. (2016a). Access to art and materials: Considerations for art therapists (Accès à l'art et aux matériaux: facteurs à prendre en compte par les art-thérapeutes). Canadian Art Therapy Association Journal, 29(2), 100–104. http://doi.org/10.1080/08322473.2016.1252996

Partridge, E. E. (2016b). Amplified voices: Art-based inquiry into elder communication (Doctoral dissertation). Notre Dame de Namur University. Retrieved September 20, 2018 from http://webinfo.ndnu.edu:8080/login?url=http://search.proquest.com.webinfo.ndnu.edu:8080/docview/1845857392?accountid=25323

Partridge, E. E. (2016c, July). Art-based identity: Professionalism and expressivity. Paper presented at Art Therapy: Integrating Creativity, Healing & Professionalism 47th Annual Conference. Baltimore, MD.

Partridge, E. E. (2017, November). Carving a larger space: Lessons learned from transforming a workplace role. Paper presented at Art Therapy: Traversing Landscapes of Heart & Mind. Albuquerque, NM.

Partridge, E. E. (2018, January). Creating space for ourselves in the workplace: Art therapist identity & professional development. Workshop presented for Notre Dame de Namur Continuing Education. Belmont, CA.

Perepezko, K., Pontone, G., & Minton, L. (2018). A mind guide to Parkinson's disease. Miami, FL: Parkinson's Foundation.

Pike, A. A. (2013). The effect of art therapy on cognitive performance among ethnically diverse older adults. Art Therapy, 30(4), 159–168. http://doi.org/10.1080/07421656.2014.8 47049

Pizzi, M. (2001). The Pizzi Holistic Wellness Assessment. Occupational Therapy in Health Care, 13(3–4), 51–66. http://doi.org/http://dx.doi.org/10.1080/J003v13n03_06

Prigerson, H. G., Maciejewski, P. K., Reynolds, C. F. I., Bierhals, A. J., Newsom, J. T., Fasiczka, A., Frank, E., Doman, J. & Miller, M. (1995). The inventory of complicated grief: A scale to measure maladaptive symptoms of loss. Psychiatry Research, 59(1–2), 65–79.

Putnam, M. (2015). Replacing the elderly with older adults in JGSW publications. Journal of Gerontological Social Work, 58(3), 229–231. http://doi.org/10.1080/01634372.201 5.1033363

Quoidbach, J., Gruber, J., Mikolajczak, M., Kogan, A., Kotsou, I., & Norton, M. I. (2014). Emodiversity and the emotional ecosystem. Journal of Experimental Psychology: General, 143(6), 2057–2065. http://doi.org/10.1037/a0038025

Regev, D., Kurt, H., & Snir, S. (2016). Silence during art therapy: The art therapist's perspective. International Journal of Art Therapy: Inscape, 21(3), 86–94. http://doi.org/10.1080/1 7454832.2016.1219754

Roets-Merken, L. M., Zuidema, S. U., Vernooij-Dassen, M. J. F. J., & Kempen, G. I. J. M. (2014). Screening for hearing, visual and dual sensory impairment in older adults using behavioural cues: A validation study. International Journal of Nursing Studies, 51(11), 1434–1440. http://doi.org/10.1016/j.ijnurstu.2014.02.006

Rolston, B. (2003). Changing the political landscape: Murals and transition in Northern Ireland. Irish Studies Review, 11(1), 3–16. http://doi.org/10.1080/0967088032000057861

Rossetto, E. (2012). A hermeneutic phenomenological study of community mural making and social action art therapy. Art Therapy: Journal of the American Art Therapy Association, 29(1), 19–26. http://doi.org/10.1080/07421656.2012.648105

Rugh, M. M. (2001). Art, nature, and aging: A shamanic perspective. In M. Farrelly-Hansen & M. Franklin (Eds.), Spirituality and art therapy: Living the connection (pp. 159–181). Philadelphia, PA: Jessica Kingsley Publishers.

Saunders, G. H., & Echt, K. V. (2007). An overview of dual sensory impairment in older adults: Perspectives for rehabilitation. Trends in Amplification, 11(4), 243–258. http://doi.org/10.1177/1084713807308365

Senie, H., & Webster, S. (Eds.). (1998). Critical issues in public art: Content, context, and controversy. Washington, DC: Smithsonian Institution Press.

Shaw, G. (2006). Patients at an exhibition. Neurology Now, (December), 28–30.

Shebib, B. (2010). Choices: Interviewing and counselling skills for Canadians (4th ed.). Toronto, Canada: Pearson Education Canada. http://doi.org/9780135074558

Smith, M. (2017, November 16). Brave new art world: The app that brings galleries into your living room. The Guardian. Retrieved September 20, 2018 from www.theguardian. com/small-business-network/2017/nov/16/brave-new-art-world-the-app-that-brings-galleries-into-your-living-room

Span, P. (2011, May 31). Mean girls in assisted living. New York Times. Retrieved September 20, 2018 from https://newoldage.blogs.nytimes.com/2011/05/31/mean-girls-in-the-nursing-home/?_r=0

Spaniol, S. (2005). "Learned hopefulness": An arts-based approach to participatory action research. Art Therapy, 22(2), 86–91. http://doi.org/10.1080/07421656.2005.10129 446

Stephenson, R. C. (2010). The creative experience of women: Art making and old age. New York, NY: New York University.

Stephenson, R. C. (2014). Art in aging: How identity as an artist can transcend the challenges of aging. Creativity and Human Development, (5), 1–18.

Steptoe, A., & Wardle, J. (2017). Life skills, wealth, health, and wellbeing in later life. Proceedings of the National Academy of Sciences, 114(17), 4354–4359. http://doi.org/10.1073/pnas.1616011114

Stewart, E. G. (2004). Art therapy and neuroscience blend: Working with patients who have dementia. Art Therapy, 21(3), 148–155. http://doi.org/10.1080/07421656.2004.10129499

Strout, K. A., David, D. J., Dyer, E. J., Gray, R. C., Robnett, R. H., & Howard, E. P. (2016). Behavioral interventions in six dimensions of wellness that protect the cognitive health of community-dwelling older adults: A systematic review. Journal of the American Geriatrics Society, 64(5), 944–958. http://doi.org/10.1111/jgs.14129

Sturm, V. E., McCarthy, M. E., Yun, I., Madan, A., Yuan, J. W., Holley, S. R., Ascher, E.A., Boxer, A.L., Miller, B.L., & Levenson, R. W. (2011). Mutual gaze in Alzheimer's disease, frontotemporal and semantic dementia couples. Social Cognitive and Affective Neuroscience, 6, 359–367. http://doi.org/10.1093/scan/nsq055

Sweetland, J., & Volmert, A. (2017). Finding the frame: An empirical approach to reframing aging and ageism. Washington, DC: FrameWorks Institute. Retrieved September 20, 2018 from http://frameworksinstitute.org/assets/files/aging_elder_abuse/aging_research_report_final_2017.pdf

The I'm Still Here Foundation. (n.d.). ARTZ: Artists for Alzheimer's. Retrieved May 3, 2015, from www.programsforelderly.com/memory-artz-artists-for-alzheimers.php

Theisen, O. J. (2010). Walls that speak: The murals of John Thomas Biggers. Denton, TX: University of North Texas Press.

Thomas, W. (1996). Life worth living: How someone you love can still enjoy life in a nursing home: The Eden Alternative in action. St. Louis, MO: VanderWyk & Burnham.

Thomas, W. (2006). In the arms of elders: A parable of wise leadership and community building. St. Louis, MO: VanderWyk & Burnham.

Thompson, N. (2015). Seeing power: Art and activism in the 21st century. Brooklyn, NY: Melville House.

Timm-Bottos, J. (2016). Beyond counseling and psychotherapy, there is a field. I'll meet you there. Art Therapy, 33(3), 160–162. http://doi.org/10.1080/07421656.2016.1199248

Trzaska, J. D. (2012). The use of a group mural project to increase self-esteem in high-functioning, cognitively disabled adults. The Arts in Psychotherapy, 39(5), 436–442. http://doi.org/10.1016/j.aip.2012.06.003

United Nations Department of Economic and Social Affairs Population Division. (2017). World population prospects: The 2017 revision, key findings and advance tables. Working Paper No. ESA/P/WP/248. Retrieved September 20, 2018 from https://esa.un.org/unpd/wpp/Publications/Files/WPP2017_KeyFindings.pdf

van Dulmen, S., Smits, L., & Eide, H. (2017). Filling in memory gaps through emotional communication; promising pathways in caring for persons with dementia. Patient Education and Counseling, 100(11), 2121–2124. http://doi.org/10.1016/j.pec.2017.06.014

Verity, J. (2007). The bus stop band-aid. Retrieved March 30, 2018, from https://dementiacareinternational.com/2007/02/the-bus-stop-band-aid

Wadeson, H. (2003). Making art for professional processing. Art Therapy: Journal of the American Art Therapy Association, 20(4), 208–218.

Waller, D. (2002). Arts therapies and progressive illness: Nameless dread. New York, NY: Brunner-Routledge.

Weiss, J. (1984). Expressive therapy with elders and the disabled: Touching the heart of life. New York, NY: Haworth Press.

White, V. E. (2002). Developing counseling objectives and empowering clients: A strength-based intervention. Journal of Mental Health Counseling, 24(3), 270–279. Retrieved September 20, 2018 from www.thefreelibrary.com/Developing+counseling+objectives+and+empowering+clients:+a...-a090393248

Williams, C. L., Newman, D., & Hammar, L. M. (2018). Preliminary study of a communication intervention for family caregivers and spouses with dementia. International Journal of Geriatric Psychiatry, 33(2), e343–e349. http://doi.org/10.1002/gps.4816

Williams, K. (2013). Evidence-based strategies for communicating with older adults in long-term care. Journal of Clinical Outcomes Management, 20(11), 507–512.

Williams, K., Kemper, S., & Hummert, M. L. (2003). Improving nursing home communication: An intervention to reduce elderspeak. The Gerontologist, 43(2), 242–247.

Woywood, C., & Davenport, M. (2013). Remembering through art: Imaginative reconstructions with older adults experiencing dementia. Journal of Art for Life, 4(1). Retrieved September 20, 2018 from http://journals.fcla.edu/jafl/article/view/84238/81359

Wrzesniewski, A., Berg, J. M., & Dutton, J. E. (2010, June). Turn the job you have into the job you want. Harvard Business Review, 114–117.

Wrzesniewski, A., & Dutton, J. E. (2001). Crafting a job: Revisioning employees as active crafters of their work. Academy of Management Review, 26(2), 179–201. http://doi.org/10.2307/259118

Yeo, R., & Bolton, A. (n.d.). Disability murals. Retrieved February 22, 2015, from www.disabilitymurals.org.uk/index.php

Yeo, R., & Bolton, A. (2008). "I don't have a problem, the problem is theirs": The priorities of Bolivian disabled people in words and pictures. Leeds, UK: The Disability Press.

Yeo, R., & Bolton, A. (2013). Welcome to our world. Retrieved October 29, 2018 from www.disabilitymurals.org.uk/Disability%20Murals%20-%20shortened%20research%20summary.pdf

Zeisel, J., & Raia, P. (2000). Nonpharmacological treatment for Alzheimer's disease: A mind-brain approach. American Journal of Alzheimer's Disease and Other Dementias, 15(6), 331–340. http://doi.org/10.1177/153331750001500603

Zoellner, T. (2015). Cornell's enormous new mural depicts every living bird family. Retrieved March 16, 2018, from www.audubon.org/news/cornells-enormous-new-mural-depicts-every-living-bird-family

ABOUT THE AUTHOR

Erin Partridge, PhD, ATR-BC is an artist and board certified, registered art therapist. She lives on a ranch in Lafayette, CA. Her clinical experience includes work in community, pediatric, forensic, and geriatric settings. Erin received a BFA, studying fine art, psychology, and women's studies at Cal Poly, San Luis Obispo. She went on to obtain an MA in art therapy from New York University in 2008, and a PhD in art therapy from Notre Dame de Namur (NDNU) in 2016.

Erin's teaching and lecturing experience includes teaching at NDNU in the art therapy department, guest lectures in art and counseling programs, mentoring undergraduate and graduate students, workshop facilitation at conferences, and interviews with media about art therapy. Her clinical experience includes work in community, pediatric, forensic, and geriatric settings, and she has published in the areas of art therapy, elder care, community-based research, and technology. She is currently working on responding to the findings of her research within the elder care context, and conducting continued research in this setting. She is also working on the use of art therapy in workplace settings as a way to increase creativity and innovation. Her research interests incorporate the lived experience and focus on participatory, ethnographic, and art-based approaches.

SUBJECT INDEX

Page numbers followed by lower-
case *f* indicate figures.

access to art 111
accordion bound books 35, 37–8
ageism 17, 18, 25–6, 79–81, 93, 118
aging process 14, 15, 17–18, 50–1, 58,
    81–2, 109
Alzheimer's disease 16
American Geriatrics Society 20
Amplified Voices study 91–6
anger 34
anhedonia 39, 40
anxiety
    connecting beyond diagnoses 62, 66
    difficult family news 77
    emodiversity 40
    health anxiety 51
    processing grief 33, 34
    release and relaxation 51, 52, 54
apps 110
"Apps for Obama" (Witten painting) 113
art discussion groups 107, 109, 111,
    112–15, 119
art display and exhibition 97–104, 108,
    110, 119
art galleries 105, 108, 111–12
art history 105–15
    art discussion groups 112–15
    overview 105
    trips to art venues 105–12
art materials *see* materials
Art Space Scoring Grid 125–6
art students 83, 89–91, 108
art studios 23–4
    see also open studio setting
art therapists

as fellow artists 27–8
lived experience 19–21
qualities of the facilitator 26–8
as studio assistants 27
art therapy
    art history 105–15
    and art with older adults 15–17,
        117–21
    connecting beyond diagnoses 57–70
    display and exhibition 97–104
    empowered elders 11–14
    individual art therapy 33–46
    mural projects 83–96
    open studio setting 47–56
    philosophical framework 15–31
    projects with purpose 71–82
    qualities 21–31
    reciprocal empowerment 120–1
    responding to art 114–15
    synthesis of the approaches 119–20
Art Therapy Delphi study 22
art venues, trips to 105–12
artworks by older adults 40f, 43f, 49f,
    53f, 57f, 67f, 68f, 69f, 74f, 80f, 120f
assisted living settings
    art discussion groups 114
    empowered elders 11, 14
    individual art therapy 34, 38–41, 46
    intergenerational projects 81, 90
    mural projects 90
    open studio setting 47, 48

bingo 11, 118
book form 34, 35, 36–8, 55
Boston Marathon bombing 72–4
bullying 57

camouflaged settings 84
change 22, 24
charcoal drawings 52, 53
Chast, Roz 109
clergy 68–9
cognitive impairment 55, 71, 79
collage 43–6
collage gardening 43, 43f, 44–5
collagraph images 60, 61, 67, 68f
collagraph word project 61
coloring activities 66
communication 16, 26, 91–6
community 71, 75, 76
community response directive 76
complicated grief 33–4
confidentiality 97
connectedness 72, 84, 105, 117
connecting beyond diagnoses 57–70
    dignifying the words 59–61
    example artworks 57f, 67f, 68f, 69f
    living in the after 68–70
    overview 57–9
    smallest marks 61–2
    visual impairment 63–5
    working with what is 65–8
contemporary art 113
Contemporary Jewish Museum 109
continuing education 109
cooking projects 29
Creative Aging International 15
creative arts therapies 15, 71
creativity 23–4, 26, 28, 50, 117
cultural heritage 104
curating the space 103, 104

"Dead Reckoning I" (Witten painting) 113
Death Café project 110
décor 103
dementia
    art discussion groups 113
    connecting beyond diagnoses 57, 58,
        59, 60, 61–2
    difficult family news 77, 78
    displaying art 101, 103, 104
    individual art therapy 45, 46
    intergenerational projects 79
    mural projects 83, 84, 85, 87, 88
    open studio setting 49, 51, 55
    philosophical framework 16

projects with purpose 71, 72, 77, 78,
    79
    qualities of the elders 29, 30
    qualities of the space 25
    reactions to the news 72
    self-assessing needs 18–19
    trips to art venues 107, 111–12
depression 33, 34, 40–2, 51, 63, 66
deYoung Museum 119
Dia de los Muertos 110
difficult family news 76–7
dignity 27, 62, 65
discrimination 19, 117
discussion groups 107, 109, 111,
    112–15, 119
diseases of later life 17, 18, 27, 58
displaying art 97–104, 119
drawings 52, 53, 53f, 57f, 67f, 68, 69,
    69f
dual coding theory 16
dual sensory impairment 63

Eden Alternative 18
education 109–10
elder curators 103, 104
elders
    definition 10
    empowered elders 11–14
    qualities of 22f, 29–31, 58
    see also older adults
elderspeak 25
emodiversity 39–40, 41
emotions
    aging process 110
    emodiversity 39–40, 41
    processing grief 36, 37
    reactions to the news 72, 74
    self-assessing needs 18–19
empowerment
    art and art therapy with older adults
        17, 117, 118
    art display and exhibition 97, 100
    empowered elders 11–14
    life skills 19
    mural projects 83, 84, 88
    open studio setting 47
    paper gardens 44
    projects with purpose 74
    qualities for art therapy 24, 30

reciprocal empowerment 120–1
self-assessing needs 18
end-of-life care 15, 33, 102
ethical guidelines 97
exhibition of art 97–104, 108, 110, 119
expressive therapy 16

facilitator, qualities of 22f, 26–8, 30, 33
family 12–13, 36, 76–8, 83
family memorial directive 78
fetal imagery 35–6, 37
fiber art 59
fire safety 75
forgetting 59
found-phrase poetry 14
framed images 103–4
FrameWorks Institute 17, 117

galleries 105, 108, 111–12
gardening 41–5
gestures 26, 46, 62, 92, 101, 114
graffiti 95, 109
grief 18, 28, 33–4, 36, 44, 52, 53f, 110
group dynamics 83, 100, 118

handwriting 41
happiness 19
health 18, 19, 34, 51, 58
hearing loss 63, 64, 112–13
helplessness 26, 66
heritage 104
holistic wellness 19, 90, 117
hospice care 102
Houlding, Jesse 60
House of Memories program 111
humor 50, 58, 69

identity 19, 37, 51, 64, 69, 70, 104
implicit memory 24
independence 12, 41, 55
independent living 41, 103
individual art therapy 33–46
assisted living 38–41
example artworks 40f, 43f
overview 33
paper gardens 41–5
processing grief 33–8
words as record of life 45–6
infantilization 25, 74

inflammation 40
inspiration points 25–6, 33, 114
intergenerational projects 79–82, 88,
89–91, 120
interpersonal dynamics 54–5

job crafting 118

Kim, Jane 119, 120
kinetic processes 60
Kramer, Edith 26

Lawrence, Jacob 114
learned helplessness 26
learning 16
lectures 112
life expectancy 21
life skills 19
lived experience 19–21, 29
loss 28, 34, 36, 110

macular degeneration 63, 64
materials
individual art therapy 33, 34–5
open studio setting 47, 48
qualities for art therapy 23, 24, 25,
28, 30, 59
meals 29
medical care 15
medical confidentiality 97
memorials 75, 99, 103
memory 16, 17, 24, 27, 59, 60, 104
memory care settings
difficult family news 76–7
displaying art 104
materials 25
mural projects 84, 86, 88
qualities of the elders 30
reactions to the news 72–4
trips to art venues 111
mild cognitive impairment 71, 79
mobility issues 85
modified accordion bound books 37–8
mural projects 83–96
Amplified Voices study 91–6
art therapist lived experience 20, 21
as camouflage or stimulus 84
intergenerational projects 89–91
overview 83–4

mural projects *cont.*
    painting process 86–9
    public art 109
    synthesis of the approaches 119
    as welcome 84–6
museums 81, 105–11
music 65

nature 44–5, 87–8
neuroscience 16
new media 28
new museology movement 104
news
    community response directive 76
    difficult family news 76–7
    reactions to the news 72–6
non-verbal communication 16, 26, 27, 78

Oakland Museum of California 110
O'Keefe, Georgia 39
Oldenburg, Claes 112
Older Adult Is Scale, An 124
older adults
    art and art therapy 15–17, 117–21
    art discussion groups 112–15
    art display and exhibition 97–104
    art history 105–15
    art therapist lived experience 19–21
    artworks 40*f*, 43*f*, 49*f*, 53*f*, 57*f*, 67*f*,
        68*f*, 69*f*, 74*f*, 80*f*, 120*f*
    connecting beyond diagnoses 57–70
    definition 10
    elder curators 103
    empowered elders 11–14
    individual art therapy 33–46
    intergenerational projects 79–82,
        89–91
    mural projects 83–96
    An Older Adult Is Scale 124
    open studio setting 47–56
    participation rubric 123
    philosophical framework 15–31
    projects with purpose 71–82
    qualities for art therapy 21–31
    qualities of the elders 22*f*, 29–31, 58
    reciprocal empowerment 120–1
    shifting ideas about 17–19
    society view of 79–80, 81–2

open studio setting 47–56
    art therapy 49–54
    difficult interpersonal dynamics 54–5
    example artworks 49*f*, 53*f*
    gallery visits 108
    individual art therapy 39
    living studio 56
    overview 47–8
    qualities of the space 23
    working with what is 66

painting
    art discussion groups 113–14
    connecting beyond diagnoses 62–5,
        67, 69
    displaying art 98, 100
    example artworks 49*f*, 67*f*, 69*f*, 74*f*
    individual art therapy 45
    mural projects 84–5
    watercolor painting 45, 49, 64, 98
paint pens 84–5
paper collagraph technique 60
paper gardens 41–5
Parkinson's disease 57, 65–6, 67
participation rubric 123
passivity 26, 44, 49
philosophical framework 15–31
    art and art therapy with older adults
        15–17
    art therapist lived experience 19–21
    overview 15
    qualities for art therapy 21–31
    shifting ideas about older adults
        17–19
photographs 36, 39, 77, 78, 87, 100,
    108
poetry 14, 51, 114
Pop Art 112
posture 92
power 55
procedural memory 24
progressive illnesses 66
project guidance
    collage gardening 44–5
    collagraph word project 61
    community response directive 76
    family memorial directive 78
    modified accordion bound book 37–8

projects with purpose 71–82
    community response directive 76
    difficult family news 76–7
    example artworks 74*f*, 80*f*
    family memorial directive 78
    intergenerational projects 79–82
    overview 71
    reactions to the news 72–6
prompts 104
protests 74, 75
public art 108
public memorials 75
purpose, sense of 62, 71, 79

qualities of the elders 22*f*, 29–31, 33, 58
qualities of the facilitator 22*f*, 26–8, 33
qualities of the space 22*f*, 23–6, 30,
    33–5, 47–8, 66
quality of life 63, 66

reality checks 77
reciprocal empowerment 120–1
rehabilitation work 117
relationships 16
repetition in art 60
representational art 98, 113
research projects 19–21, 22
resilience 28, 33, 54, 74, 111
resources 10, 123–6
responding to art 114–15
retirement 33, 34, 35, 37, 41, 69–70
rituals 24

safety 25, 27, 30
scenic drives 83, 91, 92, 94–5
self-assessment 18, 19
sensory impairment 63, 113
sexism 93
sight impairment 13, 63–5, 103, 109,
    113
silence, working with 30, 112
skilled nursing settings 17, 62, 119
slide shows 110
smart phone apps 110
social aesthetics 29
social connectedness 72, 84, 105
social justice 71, 84
space, qualities of 22*f*, 23–6, 30, 33–5,
    47–8, 66

speech difficulties 58
staff engagement 109
stigma 19, 34, 57
storytelling 89, 95, 104
street art 84–5, 95
stress 28, 66
strokes 41, 57, 58
students 89–91, 108
studios 23–4
    see also open studio setting
successful aging 18
suicidal ideation 34, 38
supplies *see* materials
symptom assessment 18

tables 48
tactile art processes 101
teaching artist programs 16
terror attacks 72–4
Tiravanija, Rirkrit 29
touch 92, 101
trauma 51
treatment goals 83
tribute art 74
trips to art venues 105–12
    discussing art in the museum 107–8
    gallery visits 108
    museum as continuing education
        109–10
    planning a trip 106–7
    public art 109
    trips for elders with dementia 111–12
    virtual museum visits 110
trust 48, 54, 72

verbal communication 16, 26, 41, 59, 72
video shows 110
virtual museum visits 110
visual art 16, 37
visual impairment 13, 63–5, 103, 109,
    113
vocalizations 35, 46, 101

Wall of Birds (Kim mural) 119, 120
watercolor painting 45, 49, 49*f*, 64, 74*f*,
    98
weaving 55, 58–9
wellness 16, 19, 39, 71, 90, 110, 117
wire weaving 55

witness role 26, 97
Witten, Jack 113
words
    dignifying 59–61
    as record of life 45–6
workplace stress 28
work setting, choosing 11

workspaces 48
writing 40, 41

younger people 79–82, 88, 89–91

zine making 17

AUTHOR INDEX

Abraham, R. 17, 59
Abramowitz, K. 17
Adamowicz, E. 14
Allen, P. B. 26
American Psychological Association 10, 16
Anderson, T. 83
Andrew, C. 39
Annweiler, C. 18
Applegate, W. B. 10
Applewhite, A. 18, 19, 26, 117
Argue, J. 83
Armstrong, J. 107
Atkins, S. 44
Awais, Y. J. 10, 19

Baca, J. 83
Backos, A. 20, 23, 26, 28
Baker, E. L. 111
Balkin, L. "Ariella" 17
Beauchet, O. 18
Bennett, J. 83
Bennington, R. 20, 105
Benson, L. 40
Berberian, M. 83
Berg, J. M. 118
Berger, K. 63
Berger, S. 63
Berry, P. 63
Bober, S. J. 72
Bolton, A. 19, 97
Bonanno, G. A. 33
Boudreaux, E. O. 16
Bradford Dementia Group 71
Brammer, M. J. 39

Broom, R. H. 17
Brown, A. M. 21–2, 112
Brown, C. 23
Browning, C. J. 63
Buettner, L. 17
Burling, S. 55
Byers, A. 17

Camic, P. M. 17, 111
Carlton, N. 28, 110
Carolan, R. 20, 23, 26
Carstensen, L. L. 18
Cassano, G. 17
Charise, A. 17
Chast, R. 109
Cherry, K. E. 16
Chilton, G. 28, 34
Clark, D. C. 39
Clover, D. 97
Coffey, M. K. 83
Cohen-Mansfield, J. 84
Conlon, B. 83
Contemporary Jewish Museum 109
Cooper, D. 69
Cooper, M. 72
Creative Aging International 15
Cruikshank, M. 18, 29, 48, 117
Czamanski-Cohen, J. 16

Dakheel-Ali, M. 84
Davenport, M. 84
Davis, K. M. 44
Deathcafe.com 110
Deaver, S. 22
Debats, D. L. 19

Debono, S. 105
deBotton, A. 107
Deloof, J. 19
De Raedt, R. 71
Desmyter, F. 71
Diachun, L. L. 17
Dieterich-Hartwell, R. M. 66
Dissanayake, E. 35, 75
Drass, J. M. 66
Dutton, J. E. 118

Echt, K. V. 63
Eden Alternative 18
Edmunds, J. D. 28
Edwards, R. T. 18
Eekelaar, C. 17
Ehresman, C. 17, 59
Eide, H. 72
Eldon, D. 35
Eldon, K. 35
Eligon, J. 72
Elliott, E. M. 16
Erikson. J. M. 23–4
Etherington Reader, A. 20

Farhodi, F. 117
Fawcett, J. 39
Fish, B. J. 28
Foster, T. 90
Fry, P. S. 19
Funk & Wagnalls New World
    Encyclopedia 65

Gagné, J. P. 34, 113
Galbraith, A. 24, 71
Galjour, C. 90
Galoustian, G. 16
Ganga, R. N. 111
Geller, S. 17
Genzlinger, N. 113
Gerber, N. 83
Gerity, L. 28
Ghesquiere, A. 34
Gibbons, R. D. 39
Goalwin, G. 83
Gol karami, S. H. 117
Gosselin, P. A. 34, 113
Grattan, N. 60
Greenberger, A. 113

Greider, L. 111
Guggenheim 29
Gussak, D. 83

Halpern, A. R. 17
Hammar, L. M. 16
Hammond, E. C. 10
Harrison, J. 20
Harrison, S. W. 35
Haydon, A. 10
Heine, C. 63
Hensley, P. L. 33, 34
Hicks, J. L. 16
Hinz, L. D. 25
Holstein, M. B. 18
Hounsome, B. 18
Houpt, K. 17
Hubalek, S. K. 15
Huebner, B. G. 16
Huet, V. 28
Hummert, M. L. 25

I'm Still Here Foundation, The 111

Jernigan, C. 35
Jue, J. 27, 28

Kabeshova, A. 18
Kaimal, G. 66, 83
Kaiser, D. 22
Kamali, M. 117
Keedwell, P. A. 39
Kempen, G. I. J. M. 63
Kemper, S. 25
Kerchner, G. A. 34, 66
Khil, L. 63
Kincaid, C. 84
Kopytin, A. I. 44
Kreps, C. F. 104
Kurt, H. 30

Ladd, K. L. 69
Lamb, S. 18, 29
Lancioni, G. E. 17
Landgarten, H. 83
Latorre, G. 83
Launay, C. P. 18
LaVorgna-Smith, M. 28
Leverenz, J. 66

Lewis, G. 17
Liebmann, M. 83
Lingard, L. 17
Low, W. H. 83
Lu, L. 97
Lundebjerg, N. E. 10, 20

MacMichael, H. N. 28
Marshall, S. 20, 26, 30
Marx, M. S. 84
Mascia, J. 63
Mather, M. 66
Mayr, U. 18
McBee, L. 72
McKenna, K. 60
McLellan, E. 72
Menon, E. K. 37
Mensinger, J. L. 66
Merjagnan, C. 18
Merluzzi, T. V. 69
Metropolitan Museum of Art 63
Miller, L. 84
Minkler, M. 18
Minton, L. 66
Mobaraki, H. 117
Monoyios, K. 119
Moon, B. L. 97
Moon, C. 26
Morris, I. 110

National Center For Creative Aging 16
National Endowment for the Arts 16
Nayeri, F. 111
Nelson, T. D. 25
Nesselroade, J. R. 18
Newman, D. 16

Oakland Museum of California 110
O'Connor, M. G. 17
O'Neil, M. 10
Ong, A. D. 40
O'Reilly, M. F. 17
Orgeta, V. 18
Orrell, M. 18
Ottemiller, D. D. 10, 19

Paivio, A. 16
Partridge, E. E. 20, 27, 28, 34, 67, 91,
    105, 109, 113, 118

Pasupathi, M. 18
Peacock, J. R. 84
Perepezko, K. 66
Perilli, V. 17
Phillips, M. L. 39
Pike, A. A. 17
Pizzi, M. 90
Pontone, G. 66
Prigerson, H. G. 34
Putnam, M. 10

Quoidbach, J. 40, 41

Raia, P. 17
Ram, N. 40
Regev, D. 30
Roets-Merken, L. M. 63
Rolston, B. 83
Ross, D. 24
Rossetto, E. 84
Roth, A. G. 17
Rugh, M. M. 26, 44

Sadoski, M. 16
Saunders, G. H. 63
Scheftner, W. A. 39
Selma, L. 17
Senie, H. 90
Shaw, G. 111
Shebib, B. 19, 30
Singh, N. N. 17
Smith, M. 110
Smits, L. 72
Snir, S. 30
Span, P. 55
Spaniol, S. 19
Spengel, S. 90
Springham, N. 17
Steinman, B. A. 63
Stephenson, R. C. 17, 71
Steptoe, A. 19
Stewart, E. G. 17, 49
Strout, K. A. 90
Sturm, V. E. 72
Subrin, R. 24
Sweetland, J. 10, 17, 117

Thein, K. 84
Theisen, O. J. 83

Thomas, W. 18
Thompson, N. 29
Timm-Boutos, J. 17
Tischler, V. 111
Trucil, D. E. 10
Trzaska, J. D. 83

United Nations Department of Economic
   and Social Affairs Population
   Division 21

van Dulmen, S. 72
Verity, J. 84
Vernooij-Dassen, M. J. F. J. 63
Volmert, A. 10, 17, 117

Wadeson, H. 28
Waller, D. 66
Wardle, J. 19
Webster, S. 90

Weiss, J. 16
Wellmann, J. 63
Westreich, L. 72
Whelan, G. 111
White, V. E. 40
Williams, C. L. 16
Williams, K. 25, 34
Williams, L. D. 44
Williams, S. C. R. 39
Wilson, K. 111
Woods, B. 18
Woywood, C. 84
Wrzesniewski, A. 118

Yeo, R. 19, 97
Yuen, F. 97

Zautra, A. J. 40
Zeisel, J. 17
Zoellner, T. 119
Zuidema, S. U. 63